Charles II

Clare Jackson is the Senior Tutor of Trinity Hall, Cambridge University. She has presented a number of highly successful programmes on the Stuart dynasty for the BBC and is currently writing a new history of Stuart Britain during the long seventeenth century (*c.* 1580–1760)

CLARE JACKSON

Charles II
The Star King

PENGUIN BOOKS

PENGUIN BOOKS

UK | USA | Canada | Ireland | Australia
India | New Zealand | South Africa

Penguin Books is part of the Penguin Random House group of companies
whose addresses can be found at global.penguinrandomhouse.com.

First published by Allen Lane 2016
First published in Penguin Books 2018
002

Set in 9.5/13.5 pt Sabon LT Std
Typeset by Jouve (UK), Milton Keynes
Printed and bound in Great Britain by Clays Ltd, Elcograf S.p.A.

ISBN: 978–0–141–98745–3

www.greenpenguin.co.uk

MIX
Paper from
responsible sources
FSC® C018179

Penguin Random House is committed to a
sustainable future for our business, our readers
and our planet. This book is made from Forest
Stewardship Council® certified paper.

Contents

Note on the Text

In Charles II's reign, the Julian ('Old Style') calendar was in use throughout his three kingdoms of England, Scotland and Ireland; this was ten days behind the Gregorian ('New Style') calendar followed in continental Europe. In this book, 1 January is taken as the start of each year, as had been the case in Scotland since 1600, although the English New Year officially started on 25 March. In quotations from primary sources, original orthography has usually been modernized and punctuation amended.

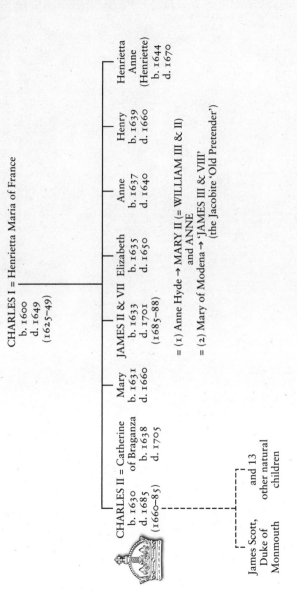

CHARLES I = Henrietta Maria of France
b. 1600
d. 1649
(1625–49)

CHARLES II = Catherine of Braganza
b. 1630   b. 1638
d. 1685   d. 1705
(1660–85)

Mary
b. 1631
d. 1660

JAMES II & VII
b. 1633
d. 1701
(1685–88)

= (1) Anne Hyde → MARY II (= WILLIAM III & II) and ANNE

= (2) Mary of Modena → 'JAMES III & VIII' (the Jacobite 'Old Pretender')

Elizabeth
b. 1635
d. 1650

Anne
b. 1637
d. 1640

Henry
b. 1639
d. 1660

Henrietta Anne (Henriette)
b. 1644
d. 1670

James Scott, Duke of Monmouth

and 13 other natural children

Charles II

I
The Star King

If you were to stop someone on the street and show them images of British monarchs through the ages, Charles II would be among the most recognizable. As the cover of this volume vividly confirms, few kings so readily embody the distinct texture of their period: for many, the 'Merry Monarch' *is* the Restoration. Lusciously flowing dark ringlets and sumptuously rich Cavalier attire evoke nostalgic impressions of baroque theatricality, swashbuckling extravagance and sexual innuendo. In popular memory, costume dramas and romantic fiction, Charles is affectionately remembered as one of this country's most charismatic and affable monarchs. He was that rare phenomenon: a king with real star quality.

Precisely because of this correlation, however, few monarchs have acquired so polarized a posthumous reputation. Scholarly opinion has preserved a more equivocal distance, refusing to be seduced by this king's popular appeal. To aspiring biographers, Charles presents a challenge, having repeatedly evaded attempts to capture his personality. Since contemporary accounts of his character yield only a prevailing 'feeling of unreachability', frustrated historians have reluctantly concluded that 'the man inside the king eluded the observer'.[1] In 1683, the cleric Gilbert Burnet described Charles as having 'the greatest art of concealing himself of any man alive', making it impossible for courtiers to gauge his reactions, while John Sheffield, Duke of Buckingham, considered him 'full of dissimulation and very adroit at it'.[2] Depicted as 'the most slippery of kings', Charles has been labelled by modern scholars as 'the master of the mixed signal' and a man who 'schooled himself to become an enigma'.[3] The notion of revealing a single 'true' self might, however, have been deemed naïvely reductionist by Charles himself. As a former confidant, George Savile, Marquis of Halifax, recalled in a posthumous character sketch, Charles would often instinctively pit his 'personal against his political capacity' and speak 'most dexterously against himself', insisting – in a moment of brilliantly self-aware duality – that 'Charles Stuart would be bribed against the King', though Halifax added that he tended to cleave 'more to his natural self' than to his official role as monarch.[4]

This biography emphasizes instead the vital importance that Charles attached to popular perceptions and public representations of his kingship. No other monarch in British history has succeeded as king after a republican experiment. No other monarch was thus so acutely aware of the extent to which, following a largely peaceful restoration to his English, Scottish and Irish thrones in 1660, his survival as monarch depended on his subjects' goodwill after two traumatic decades that had seen prolonged and bloody civil wars, culminating in his father's execution, and a period of republican and military rule dominated by

Oliver Cromwell. Eschewing a conventional cradle-to-grave approach, this biography supplies a succinct chronological narrative in Chapter 2, followed by four chapters focusing on visual, ceremonial, literary and posthumous depictions of Charles II. This thematic approach reflects not only this particular monarch's preoccupations, but also our own modern obsessions with external appearance and presentational spin.

An appreciation of this king's performance is thus key to probing his personality. Indeed, as an avid supporter of Restoration theatre, Charles was adept at donning different roles, of which being monarch was just one. As an eight-year-old, he had been advised by his governor, William Cavendish, Earl of Newcastle, that a 'king must know at what time to play the king, and when to qualify it' and, during the civil wars, Charles preserved his life precisely by disguising his identity and successfully impersonating his humblest subjects while on the run from Parliamentarian enemies.[5] Moreover, at the Restoration, Charles's image became central to reasserting royal authority and to reconstituting monarchical culture more widely. Accordingly, he remains one of the most frequently depicted monarchs in British history before the advent of modern photography and film, with many more portraits, prints and sculptures surviving of Charles II than of his father, despite the cult of martyrdom that attached to Charles I after his execution in 1649. Posterity's appreciation of Charles II is also necessarily refracted through his public persona and the observations of others since he left no published writings or diaries and few personal letters, unlike his father or his grandfather James I and VI.

To get to know this king, therefore, readers need to recognize the sheer instability of Charles II's world. Unpredictability hung in the air of Restoration Britain and little could be taken at face value or guaranteed as permanent. A pervasive mood of 'secrecy, deception and equivocation' meant that even ostensibly devout Anglicans were suspected of being covert papists; parliamentary grants to wage war against France were raised while Charles simultaneously negotiated with the French court for clandestine financial subsidies in return for avoiding war; government spies posed as common highwaymen; and the debauched excesses of Charles's aristocratic court threatened to eclipse traditionally plebeian sexual mores.[6]

Charles's claim to be the 'Star King' derives, however, from the very day of his birth, 29 May 1630, when a brilliant star shone brightly in the daytime skies over London. The star – now thought to be either the planet Venus or the remnants of a supernova – was hailed as a significant portent, equivalent to the star that heralded Christ's birth in St Matthew's Gospel and led the biblical Magi to Bethlehem. As the poet Robert Herrick confirmed:

> At Noone of Day was seene a silver Star,
> Bright as the Wise-mens torch, which guided them
> To Gods sweet Babe, when borne at Bethlehem.[7]

The cosmological symbolism that had accompanied the birth of the heir to the throne and the parallels with the

Nativity were later widely celebrated at his restoration. When, for example, Sir Audley Mervin delivered his first speech as Speaker of the Irish House of Commons on 11 May 1661, he insisted that, during the civil wars, Charles had been 'wrapped up in the swaddling bands of majesty' and thereafter 'laid in a manger' during his years in exile. Mervin regretted that more 'Wise Men' had not followed a guiding 'star over the place' where Charles was residing, since that would have hastened Charles's restoration as king.[8] That same year, a painting by the Edinburgh-trained artist John Michael Wright was commissioned to hang from the ceiling of the royal bedchamber at Whitehall Palace. Entitled *Astraea Returns to Earth: The Apotheosis of Charles II*, it depicts the eponymous 'star maiden' of Greek mythology returning to earth at the dawn of a new golden age and pointing to the brilliant daytime star that had shone at Charles's birth.

The star motif also became an iconic representation of Charles's majesty through his membership of the Order of the Garter – the oldest knightly Order in Europe. From his installation as a knight in 1638, a week before his eighth birthday, Charles wore the Garter Jewels continually in adult life and used membership of the Order to maintain his chivalric status during his years in exile on the continent when the office of monarchy had been abolished in England. While Charles was temporarily resident in Jersey in September 1649 – eight months after his father's execution – an islander recalled an encounter with him, in which he was wearing plain, dark purple mourning dress, the only embellishment being a bright 'silver star'

on the left side of his cloak.[9] As king, Charles also undertook extensive building works at Windsor Castle during
the 1670s, erecting a new 'Star Building' with a twelve-
foot-high gilt star on its exterior that was designed to
create a shimmering golden reflection in the River Thames
beneath.

Fittingly, Charles himself was not only a keen amateur
astronomer, but also founded the Royal Observatory on
Greenwich Hill in 1675 – designed by Christopher Wren,
with Sir John Flamsteed appointed as the first Astronomer
Royal – with the aim of obtaining observations that could
determine terrestrial longitude and thereby equip Royal
Navy ships with better celestial charts. But the grandeur
of the Observatory's main 'Great Star Room', as it was
originally called, ultimately belied its usefulness for tran-
sit observations, as the building had a fixed roof and
proved to be incorrectly sited. More widely, appeals to
astrology and popular prognostications invariably accompanied scientific observations. Addressing the English
Parliament in September 1660, Lord Chancellor Edward
Hyde confirmed Charles's support for disbandment of the
Parliamentarian army and a general indemnity for past
actions on the grounds that the violent events of the previous two decades had 'proceeded from the ill influence of
a malignant star'; with the king's return, however, 'our
own good old stars govern us again'.[10] Four years later,
in December 1664, although cloudy weather frustrated
Charles's own attempts to view a 'blazing star' – or comet –
he hoped that its timely appearance nevertheless augured

well for his intended attacks on the Dutch fleet. From Paris, his sister Henriette sent news of the star's reception, reporting that 'all the wise men . . . and all the foolish ones too' attended viewings at the Jesuits' Observatory, prompting extensive disagreement about the comet's composition since 'no two of them think alike!'[11]

If Charles's interest in comets, shooting stars and other features of the night sky seems appropriate for a monarch often described as elusive, shadowy and evanescent, equally fitting symbolism could be drawn from the dazzling luminosity of all stars, including the one closest to us: the sun. Indeed, throughout his reign, Charles was consistently suspected of trying to emulate, if not to eclipse, his powerful younger cousin Louis XIV of France, who self-consciously ruled as the 'Sun King'. In the punning panegyric that accompanied his restoration, Charles was thus acclaimed as both a worthy 'son' and heir to his executed father and as an allegorical 'sun' to his subjects. Two generations earlier, his grandfather James I and VI had insisted that monarchs acquired their God-given glory 'to glister and shine' and serve as 'bright lamps' to illuminate their subjects' paths.[12] Observing the king's coronation in April 1661, an orphan from Christ's Hospital School described Charles II as 'so glorious a sun' and admitted that such majesty 'may well dazzle the eyes of so poor a nothing as I'.[13] On a personal level, Charles possessed abundant charisma: a word only recently coined in seventeenth-century England and which retained notions of special gifts that were divinely endowed. As Charles's physician, Dr Walter Charleton, insisted in 1661, so compelling were 'the beams of Majesty' that no one ever departed down-hearted from Charles's presence, while a Parisian doctor, Charles Patin, following a private audience with the king in the mid 1670s, reported how 'in that glorious moment, I perceived the hero before the monarch'. Patin's familiarity with the glittering brilliance of Louis XIV's court notwithstanding, he deemed Charles II 'truly rare' among monarchs in that 'the merits of his person give out more light than the splendour of majesty which surrounds them'.[14]

The 'Star King' would not, however, become the 'Sun King'. Even if Louis XIV's dictum was apocryphal, Charles cannot be imagined asserting personal ownership of his kingdoms in terms of 'l'état, c'est à moi' – and nor would his subjects have wished him to do so. In 1660, the inhabitants of the British Isles had just endured twenty traumatic years of civil warfare, constitutional upheaval and religious radicalism. Deeply traumatized, the Restoration generation has been described as recurrently 'susceptible to both nostalgia on the one hand, and nightmares on the other'.[15] Dexterity, charisma and shrewdness would be required to handle this volatile inheritance, and while Charles possessed all these qualities, he also proved himself both a lucky king and a king skilled in creating his own luck. In a play first performed in 1939, George Bernard Shaw imagined Charles II predicting that his brother and successor, James, aimed 'to be the English Louis, the British Roi Soleil, the sun king', before warning that 'this is a deuced foggy climate for sun kings, Jamie'.[16]

Throughout his life, Charles outran his enemies, outwitted his opponents, seduced his mistresses and – unlike his father and brother – retained his thrones. Dying of natural causes in his royal bedroom at Whitehall in 1685, aged fifty-four, he had good reason to thank his lucky stars.

2
Life

Born at St James's Palace at Westminster on 29 May 1630, Charles was the first surviving son and heir to Charles I and his French Catholic wife, Henrietta Maria. He was delivered by Madame Peronne – personal midwife to his maternal grandmother, Marie de' Medici – whose return journey to Paris was disrupted when she, together with her accompanying dwarf and a dancing master, were captured by Flemish pirates in the Channel and only released after a ransom was paid. The young prince was christened by Bishop William Laud of London on 27 June. His godparents comprised his uncle Louis XIII of France, his grandmother Marie de' Medici (mother of Louis) and Charles I's brother-in-law Frederick V, the beleaguered titular Elector Palatine and King of Bohemia, on whose behalf English forces had become involved in the Thirty Years War. Charles's safe arrival nevertheless lessened the dynastic need to continue supporting the Bohemian cause, provoking dismay among militant Protestants who had hoped that the Stuart dynasty might ultimately revert to the descendants of the Calvinist Frederick. Across Catholic Europe, however, Charles's arrival was welcomed with celebratory bonfires in the courtyards of Habsburg royal palaces, while the English ambassador in Madrid was honoured at a public bullfight. At home, Charles was the first prince born as heir to all three crowns of England, Scotland and Ireland, while it was nearly a century since the English had last welcomed a male heir to the throne in the person of Henry VIII's son, Edward VI. In due course, Charles I and Henrietta Maria also produced an extensive number of spare Stuart heirs: a daughter, Mary, in 1631; a son, James, Duke of York, in 1633; two further daughters, Elizabeth and Anne, in 1635 and 1637; another son, Henry, Duke of Gloucester, in 1639; and finally another daughter, Henrietta Anne ('Henriette'), in 1644.

Charles's early years, like those of his siblings, were spent mostly at Richmond Palace, several miles west of his parents' sophisticatedly baroque court at Whitehall. A royal chaplain, Brian Duppa, was appointed as Charles's tutor in 1635 and, on his eighth birthday, the prince's household was separately established under William Cavendish, Earl of Newcastle, who wrote to Charles shortly after his appointment as the prince's governor, endorsing a style of education that prioritized practicalities and eschewed scholastic pedantry. 'I would rather have you study things than words,' Newcastle advised Charles, counselling him not to 'take heed of too much book' since 'known bookworms' rarely became effective statesmen. His warning against 'Bible-mad' individuals, alerting Charles I's son to the fate of ill-advised monarchs who 'in seeming to gain the throne of Heaven, have lost their own', reflected a nervousness about religious politics in 1638 that would later prove prophetic.[1]

Charles's childhood was, however, prematurely cut short when his father's royal authority started to disintegrate, first in Scotland and subsequently in Ireland and England. Opposition to a new Scottish Prayer Book – deemed unacceptably 'popish' in form and content – unleashed the 'Bishops' Wars', and leaving his son at Whitehall Palace, Charles I spent the summers of 1639 and 1640 fighting Scottish 'Covenanters' whose resistance to royal religious policy was enshrined in a 'National Covenant' drawn up in 1638. In May 1641, the ten-year-old prince unsuccessfully attempted to plead in the House of Commons to save the life of Charles I's former associate, Thomas Wentworth, Earl of Strafford, despite his father having signed a bill of attainder against Strafford, while Newcastle was dismissed as the prince's governor after becoming implicated in a plot to rescue Strafford from the Tower of London. As relations between crown and Parliament deteriorated, Charles I sent his wife to safety on the continent in February 1642 and, after a threatened custody battle with Parliament over his eldest son, admitted to his adviser Edward Hyde that having 'gotten Charles, I care not what answer' was returned regarding MPs' subsequent demands.[2]

For the next three years, Charles was almost constantly in his father's company on campaign, covering nearly a thousand miles in 1642 alone and witnessing major pitched battles between Royalist and Parliamentarian troops, such as the encounter at Edgehill. Based in a relocated royal court in Oxford, Charles sat in a reconvened 'House of Lords' in the university's lecture hall and, together with his brother James, received an MA from the university in January 1644. By early 1645, however, the king decided to create a separate focus for Royalist activities around his eldest son, indicating to Hyde that it was 'now time to unboy him, by putting him into some action'.[3] In March, the fourteen-year-old Charles was given nominal command of the Royalist war effort in the West Country and, leaving Oxford for Bristol, never saw his father again. Following the king's heavy defeat at the Battle of Naseby in June, south-western towns including Bath, Bridgwater and Sherborne quickly fell to Parliamentarian forces and the prince retreated to Pendennis Castle in Cornwall. Shortly after Naseby, Charles I wrote to his son insisting that, in the event of his own capture, the prince should not submit to 'any conditions that are dishonourable, unsafe for your person, or derogatory to royal authority'; rather, if Charles upheld his father's dignity, he would 'make me die cheerfully, praising God for giving me so gallant a son'.[4]

Fleeing the Parliamentarian advance, Charles left mainland Britain in March 1646 and initially stayed on the Scilly Isles, before moving to Jersey where he remained until June with an entourage of around three hundred, including Hyde. Following his father's surrender to the Scottish Covenanters, Charles joined his mother at the French court, where diplomatic protocol was set aside, allowing him to be treated on terms of equal respect by his cousin Louis XIV, eight years his junior, whose minority rule as French king had started in 1643. Charles and his mother were joined in April 1648 by Charles's brother James, who had escaped Parliamentarian custody and, amid abortive plans for Royalist invasions, Charles moved to The Hague to stay with his sister Mary, Princess of Orange. As it became increasingly likely that Parliament would place his father on trial, Charles appealed to the French court to intervene but, on 4 February 1649, he received a newsletter from London reporting that the king had been publicly executed five days earlier. When he was then addressed as 'Your Majesty', Charles 'burst into tears' as all the 'ideals, loyalties, responsibilities, and dilemmas which had confounded and killed his father . . . crashed on to his eighteen-year-old shoulders'.[5]

Although the English Parliament swiftly abolished both the institution of monarchy and the House of Lords, when news reached Edinburgh of Charles I's execution, on 5 February, the Scottish Parliament instantly proclaimed Charles II King of Scotland, England and Ireland in succession to his father. While hostility to the latter's imposition of the Scottish Prayer Book had been the fatal spark that had subsequently ignited opposition throughout Britain, the Scots' attachment to their native Stuart dynasty remained unshakeable. Debating the relative advantages of joining either Irish Catholic or Scottish Presbyterian forces hostile to the English Parliament, Charles and his entourage left The Hague and wandered uncertainly to Antwerp, Brussels and Saint-Germain-en-Laye, outside Paris. After another sojourn on Jersey, the exiled court returned to Breda in the Dutch Republic for discussions involving Scottish emissaries with whom Charles decided to conclude terms.

Arriving off the Scottish coast in June 1650, Charles put

his signature to two documents that his father had stead-fastly refused to sign – the Scottish National Covenant (1638) and Solemn League and Covenant (1643) – which thereby committed him to establishing Presbyterianism in all three kingdoms. In later years, the MP for Aberdeen Alexander Jaffray rued how 'that poor young prince' had been obliged by the Scots delegation to swear an oath 'which we knew . . . he hated in his heart', concluding that '*our* sin was more than *his*'.[6] In September, Charles was reminded by a prominent Presbyterian, Robert Douglas, of the seriousness of the Covenant's obligations and warned of suspicions that 'self-interest and gaining of a crown have been more in your eye than the advancing of religion and righteousness'.[7] Kept under uncomfortable scrutiny by his Scottish hosts – and repeatedly exhorted to repent pub-licly for his own sins and those of his family – Charles even attempted escape and spent several nights sleeping rough in Glen Clova, before becoming the last monarch to be crowned in Scotland, at a ceremony at Scone Palace on 1 January 1651. In his coronation sermon, Douglas again impressed on Charles that, as a Covenanted king, he was obliged to promote Presbyterianism and, in the event of any attempt to disregard 'the very fundamentals of this contract and covenant', his subjects 'may and ought to resist by arms'.[8]

Charles's main aim in going to Scotland – to raise a Royal-ist force to invade England – was eventually achieved by the summer of 1651, but his advance was humiliatingly terminated by a comprehensive defeat at Worcester on 3 Sep-tember, when his army of 12,000 soldiers was trounced by Oliver Cromwell's force of 28,000 Parliamentarians. Imprisoned in Chester, one Royalist soldier, William Ellison, wrote to Hyde shortly afterwards, admiring the young king's courage under fire and insisting that 'certainly a braver prince never lived'. According to Ellison, Charles had supplied an inspirational example at Worcester, riding from one regiment to another to offer encouragement, 'calling every officer by his name' and constantly displaying 'so much steadiness of mind and undaunted courage in such continual danger'.[9] Having fled the carnage, the twenty-one-year-old monarch then spent forty-three nights on the run, travelling clandestinely through Bromsgrove, Stratford-upon-Avon, Cirencester, Somerset, Bridport, Brighton and Shoreham, before securing a passage to Fécamp, on the Normandy coast, where he arrived on 16 October. Relying on the repeated loyalty, courage and discretion of ordinary subjects to evade his captors, Charles famously spent the day after the battle sheltering in an oak tree in Boscobel Wood. Eventually becoming part of Restoration folklore, the king's dramatic flight from Worcester was an experience that both inspired and haunted him for the rest of his life. Even before Charles's final return from exile, the Convention Parliament had decreed that his birthday, 29 May, should be permanently preserved as a day of thanksgiving. Popularly known as 'Royal Oak Day' or 'Oak Apple Day', the anniversary was a British public holiday until 1859, while 'The Royal Oak' remains the third most popular pub name in England.[10]

For the next nine years, Charles's life in exile was characterized by itinerancy and impoverishment and by factionalism among his dispirited advisers. Indeed, the peripatetic nature of his existence is epitomized by the royal bed: ingeniously designed by Charles himself, it could be easily disassembled for stowing on a wheeled cart with packing cases.[11] To a great extent, the Stuarts became pawns of international diplomacy as long-running Franco-Spanish hostilities determined the exiled court's relative attractiveness or unacceptability to potential foreign allies. As the French court inclined towards an anti-Spanish alliance with the English Republic, Charles was obliged to leave France in 1654 and moved to Germany, where he was received as a guest in Cologne and Spa by princes of the Holy Roman Empire. The fact that Charles primarily resided in Catholic territories during his exile generated widespread hope, especially among Irish Royalists, that he might follow the example of his Protestant French grandfather, Henri IV, who had converted to Catholicism in the 1590s. Yet throughout his years in exile, Charles regularly attended Anglican service, fasted weekly in his father's memory and was appalled when his mother placed his youngest brother, Henry, in a Jesuit seminary in 1654. Having arranged to remove Henry from his mother's influence, Charles warned him that if he failed to 'remember the last words of your dead father' to remain steadfastly attached to the Protestant faith, he should be prepared never to see England, or indeed his eldest brother, again.[12]

In 1654, Charles also spent a summer holiday with his sister Mary and visited Aachen, where the siblings inspected the relics of the Emperor Charlemagne and Charles wistfully compared the size of his own sword with that of his illustrious namesake. The next year, Cromwell's audacious seizure of Jamaica from Spain rendered Charles a potentially attractive ally to Felipe IV of Spain and prompted the exiled court to move to Bruges and Brussels in the Spanish Netherlands, where Charles assembled a small army of around 2,500 soldiers dependent on Spanish pay, awaiting a combination of sufficiently propitious international and domestic circumstances to attempt a Royalist invasion.

Following Cromwell's death in September 1658, the Protectorate under his eldest son, Richard, proved short-lived, as Richard not only lacked military experience, but also struggled to control Parliament. In April 1659, the English army abolished the Cromwellian Protectorate and restored the 'Rump' Parliament that had sanctioned the regicide a decade earlier. Having failed to co-ordinate a Royalist rising from Calais in August, Charles attended the Franco-Spanish peace negotiations at Fuenterrabía in Spain before returning to Brussels. As the domestic political initiative shifted to General George Monck – who had been Cromwell's military governor in Scotland – covert negotiations started with the exiled court as, ironically, Charles's restoration was ultimately facilitated by the same army that had overseen the execution of his father. In April 1660, the exiled court issued a shrewdly worded 'Declaration' from its Dutch base in Breda, confirming its urgent wish to heal 'those wounds which have so many years together been kept bleeding' and, to reassure those who feared imminent royal vengeance, by undertaking to satisfy army arrears and, where possible, extend an indemnity for past actions.[13] In the same month, fresh elections to a 'free' Convention Parliament returned a Royalist Commons majority and, by a unanimous vote in both Houses on 8 May, Charles II was declared to have been king since his father's execution. The new monarch was, however, keenly aware of the deep ideological fault-lines that divided his kingdoms. Shortly before returning to England, he wrote to Monck, expressing his gratitude for 'your very discreet conduct of this great work' in bringing together 'persons of such different humours and contrary affections'.[14] More ominously, a Parliamentarian cleric, Ralph Josselin, had privately observed, at the start of the year, 'the nation looking more to Charles Stuart, out of love to themselves not him'.[15]

On 23 May 1660, Charles left Scheveningen in the Netherlands and arrived at Dover two days later, before astutely delaying his entry into London until his thirtieth birthday on 29 May. Widely acclaimed as an event of providential deliverance, Charles's return as king generated a mood of optimistic euphoria. As the diarist John Evelyn marvelled, the monarchy's return had been achieved 'without one drop of blood and by that very army which rebelled against him'.[16] The Convention's statute confirming 29 May as an annual holiday placed an emphasis on national resurrection, describing Charles's kingdoms as 'all in a great measure newborn and raised from the dead on this most joyful day'.[17] Moreover, Charles's restoration was accompanied by a deliberate decision to erase public memory of recent trauma: his reign was deemed to have started on 30 January 1649 and events that had occurred during the previous two decades were physically expunged from official records. In May 1660, the Convention passed an Act of Free and General Pardon, Indemnity and Oblivion that avoided attributing culpability for the civil wars to any party. The premium henceforth to be placed on reconciliation was confirmed by a general pardon issued to individuals who had committed all but the most serious of crimes (such as unlicensed murder or rape and witchcraft) during the civil wars and Interregnum, and also exempting twenty-seven named regicides. Legal judgements in private cases tried under English common law were upheld, but all public acts passed since 1641 – such as parliamentary statutes – were revoked, since they lacked royal consent. In Scotland, an Act Rescissory (1661) radically annulled all legislation enacted by 'pretended Parliaments' since 1633, including those which Charles I had attended in 1648 and over which his son had likewise presided in 1650 and 1651. Addressing the English Parliament in July 1661, Charles himself exhorted MPs to 'look forward, and not backward; and never think of what is past'.[18] Several years later, another diarist, Samuel Pepys, recorded a conversation with a colleague in which both men had resolved to set aside their differences: 'just like the interstice between the death of the old and coming in of the present king, all that time is swallowed up as if it had never been'.[19]

Amnesty and amnesia were, however, easier to proclaim than to achieve. Writing to Charles in exile, his former mentor, the Earl of Newcastle, had identified the 'greatest error of state' committed by Charles's father and

grandfather as being that they had always 'rewarded their enemies, and neglected their friends'.[20] Inevitably, anxieties
quickly surfaced that the Restoration settlement risked
perpetuating wartime impoverishment of Royalists while
preserving the enrichment of erstwhile Parliamentarian
enemies, reflected in a witticism circulating at the time
that Charles had passed an act of indemnity for his enemies and an act of oblivion for his friends. Although
the monarchy's constitutional powers remained virtually
intact from the pre-civil war period, former Royalists
faced scant prospect of compensation for their extensive
losses.

Deep divisions also persisted between advocates of religious accommodation and toleration and those who wished
to restore the established Church's monopoly of lawful
worship. In his 'Declaration' from Breda, Charles had
explicitly committed himself to granting 'a liberty to ten-
der consciences', insisting that 'no man shall be disquieted
or called in question for differences of opinion in matters
of religion which do not disturb the peace of the kingdom'.[21] Although a conference at Worcester House in
October 1660 proposed a pragmatically inclusive settlement that envisaged a single Protestant church and flexible
enforcement of the law in regard to controversial forms of
religious ceremonies, the English Parliament's Corporation Act (1661) was more draconian. It obliged all holders
of public office to swear oaths of allegiance and supremacy
to the king, to denounce as illegal the taking up of arms
against him, and to renounce the Solemn League and Covenant. The following May, an Act of Uniformity required

all English clergymen to subscribe to the Book of Common Prayer and receive episcopal ordination by 24 August 1662. On that date – which also marked the ninetieth anniversary of the St Bartholomew's Day massacre of French Protestants – over nine hundred parish clergy, including a third of London's ministers, failed to comply with the Act's requirements and left their livings. Before the Act's approval, Charles had reassured MPs that perceived delays in reaching a religious settlement should not be misinterpreted: as he ironically observed, he should have 'the worst luck in the world, if, after all the reproaches of being a Papist whilst I was abroad, I am suspected of being a Presbyterian now I am come home'.[22] North of the border, legislation passed by the Scottish Parliament in 1662 imposed a re-established Episcopalian church structure on a predominantly Presbyterian population, which resulted in around 270 ministers – or a quarter of parish incumbents – being deprived of their cures for refusing to accept Episcopal collation.

To secure the restored monarchy's dynastic future, Charles contemplated different marriage options before announcing in May 1661 that he had resolved to wed the daughter of John IV of Portugal. Acknowledging the likely unpopularity of a Catholic bride, Charles warned English MPs that if he had waited to find a marriage partner who could attract universal approval, 'you would live to see me an old bachelor, which I think you do not desire to do'.[23] Forming an Anglo-Portuguese alliance that endorsed Portugal's recent independence from Spain – and which was thereby supported by Louis XIV – Charles's marriage to

Catherine of Braganza in April 1662 brought with it an attractive dowry and the trading ports of Tangier and Bombay, making Charles II's the most generous marriage settlement hitherto received by an English monarch. Meeting his twenty-four-year-old bride on her arrival at Portsmouth, the king found that Catherine could speak neither English nor French, so the couple communicated in Spanish. As Charles reported to Edward Hyde – now ennobled as the Earl of Clarendon – it was also 'happy for the honour of the nation' that the marriage had not been immediately consummated, since his fatiguing journey from London had made him 'afraid that matters would have gone very sleepily'.[24]

Although substantial, the new queen's dowry could not provide a permanent substitute for other forms of revenue and disputes over crown finance soon broke out. As early as November 1661, Charles appealed to Parliament 'to put you in mind of the crying debts which every day call upon me' and confirmed his willingness for MPs to 'make a full inspection into my revenue' and expenditure.[25] Thereafter, royal demands for increased funding became a regular leitmotif, despite the House of Commons' acceptance that the crown's peacetime costs, to govern England alone, amounted to £1.2 million, and that such a sum should be raised by taxation. In the event, however, state receipts fell far short of that figure and additional agreements regarding unpaid army arrears presented further demands.

More financial strain was placed upon Parliament by Charles's declaration of war against the Dutch in March 1665 as opposition to Dutch commercial rivalry fused with

Anglican aversion to Dutch republican government and religious toleration. Although the conflict was initially popular and opened with a rout by the English of the Dutch fleet off Lowestoft in June, subsequent defeats incurred heavy casualties and mounting expense. Dislocation arising from the war also coincided with an alarming outbreak of bubonic plague in London, the death toll for which peaked in September 1665, when over seven thousand deaths were recorded in one week alone, prompting the royal court to move from Whitehall to Hampton Court and then to Salisbury and Oxford. At the end of January 1666, Louis XIV entered the war on the Dutch side, while the conflict proved deeply unpopular in Charles's northern kingdom: denying any quarrel with the Dutch, the Scots nevertheless suffered extensive disruption to trade at a time when sectarian divisions also erupted in Lowland Scotland during the Presbyterian Covenanters' fortnight-long 'Pentland Rising' in November.

With the numeral '666' denoting the sign of the Beast in the Book of Revelation, the year's apocalyptic resonances only intensified with the Great Fire of London in September 1666. The five-day conflagration destroyed over 13,000 homes, laid waste to 400 acres of land in the City and caused damage to property and goods estimated at around £3 million. During the fire, Charles's personal courage again attracted extensive admiration, with Evelyn deeming it extraordinary to observe the king and his brother James 'labouring in person, and being present, to command, order, reward and encourage workmen; by which [the king] showed his affection to his people and gained theirs'.[26] Addressing displaced Londoners directly, Charles insisted that the fire had been from the 'hand of God', exacerbated by 'the terrible wind', thereby blaming divine displeasure, rather than a Dutch, French or more widespread Catholic conspiracy.[27] Meanwhile, as the costs of the Dutch war mounted and public opinion turned against the conflict, peace talks were initiated during which a large proportion of the English fleet was withdrawn and anchored at Chatham in Kent. In June 1667, however, a Dutch flotilla surged up the River Medway on an incoming tide and captured Sheerness. Breaking the iron chain intended to safeguard the English fleet, the Dutch sank several warships and towed two others back to Holland, including the Royal Navy's flagship, the *Royal Charles*.

Successive catastrophes of plague, fire and ignominious military defeat took their toll and rapidly reversed the initial optimism that had accompanied the Restoration. For all the euphoria that had greeted Charles on his return as king in 1660, ruling a people deeply divided by two decades of civil turmoil was always likely to be challenging. In a sermon preached on 30 January 1667, the Rector of Bath Abbey, Joseph Glanvill – also a Fellow of the Royal Society – chose an appropriately scientific metaphor to warn that a 'people that rebelled once, and successfully, will be ready to do so often', just 'as water that has been boiled, will boil again the sooner'.[28] Charles himself also became the target of mounting personal criticism for, despite having not yet produced an heir by his wife, by 1667 he had fathered at least nine illegitimate children by four different women, the majority of whom were publicly acknowledged in a way that brought inevitable humiliation for his wife, Catherine. While Charles was in exile, his eldest son, James (later Duke of Monmouth), had been born in 1649 to Lucy Walter, followed by a daughter, Charlotte (later Countess of Yarmouth), to Elizabeth Killigrew, Countess of Shannon. In 1657, he had a son, Charles (later Earl of Plymouth), by the daughter of a Derbyshire Royalist, Catherine Pegge, by whom he also had a daughter, Catherine, the following year. After the Restoration, Charles had five children by Barbara Villiers (Countess of Castlemaine and later Duchess of Cleveland): a daughter, Anne, in 1661; two sons, Charles and Henry (later Dukes of Southampton and Grafton respectively), in 1662 and 1663; followed by a daughter, Charlotte (later Countess of Lichfield), in 1664, and a son, George (later Duke of Northumberland), in 1665.

Amid an increasingly apprehensive public mood, even instinctively loyal observers like Evelyn and Pepys, walking together in Westminster Hall in April 1667, found themselves 'talking of the badness of the government, where nothing but wickedness, and wicked men and women command the king' and blaming Charles for being insufficiently principled to 'gainsay anything that relates to his pleasures'. In the 'Bawdy House Riots' that took place the following March, crowds attacked London brothels, incensed that Charles's government seemed more concerned to persecute pious Nonconformists who worshipped outside the established Anglican Church than to suppress vice and licentiousness. As Pepys recorded, the rioters reportedly 'had the confidence to say that they did ill in contenting themselves in pulling down the little bawdy-houses', regretting that they had not instead gone to 'pull down the great bawdy-house at Whitehall'.[29]

At Whitehall, Charles's long-serving political manager, the Earl of Clarendon, was impeached and exiled, ostensibly for mismanagement of the Dutch war, but having also fallen under suspicion of deliberately promoting Charles's marriage to a barren queen to promote his own family's interests via his daughter, Anne, who had married the king's brother, and heir presumptive, James, Duke of York, in 1660. The dynasty's precariousness was exposed in March 1669 when a coach transporting Charles, the Dukes of York and Monmouth and Prince Rupert of the Rhine through London at night overturned at Holborn. Although Charles escaped unhurt and poor street lighting was blamed, the accident had nevertheless threatened the king, his only surviving brother and heir presumptive, his eldest (illegitimate) son and his cousin. The fragility of the restored monarchy's fortunes was also apparent overseas. When Charles's mother died in France that September, her funeral sermon was delivered by the renowned court preacher Jacques-Bénigne Bossuet, who warned that the English people had become so 'factious, rebellious and opinionated' and 'incapable of constancy' that, after the civil wars, nothing but 'appalling precipices' could be anticipated.[30]

By the late 1660s, one potential solution to securing the succession might have been for Charles to follow Henry VIII's precedent and divorce Catherine of Braganza in order to remarry, defying any diplomatic repercussions with Portugal. Aristocratic divorce became politically prominent at this time when John Manners, Baron Roos, introduced private legislation into the House of Lords in 1670, seeking a divorce in order to remarry and sire an heir, after unexpectedly succeeding to the earldom of Rutland. Roos's bill was promoted by Bishop John Wilkins of Chester, who confirmed that divorces might be granted, both for adultery and for 'immundicity of the womb, which is given forth to be the queen's condition'.[31] Having provoked widespread surprise by deciding to attend the Lords debates in person, Charles enthusiastically proclaimed parliamentary proceedings to be 'better than going to a play' and his known support for Roos's case aided the bill's narrow victory. As the poet and MP Andrew Marvell noted in a letter to his nephew, Charles had also stated that 'he knew not why a woman might not be divorced for barrenness, as a man for impotency'.[32] Moreover, once peers became accustomed to Charles's presence at Westminster, it was alleged by Gilbert Burnet that some evidently started 'to speak with the more boldness' about politics, aware that an official ban on the publication of parliamentary debates gave them 'more liberty because what they had said could not be reported wrong'. Burnet disapproved, however, of Charles's descent into parliamentary politics, lamenting that the king thereby 'became a common solicitor, not only in public affairs, but even in private matters'.[33]

Meanwhile, on the giant chessboard of international diplomacy, Charles proved a risky and audacious strategist. In

February 1668, he entered a Triple Alliance with Sweden and his former enemy the Dutch United Provinces to try to halt French expansionism. Simultaneously, however, he fomented a plan to form a defensive alliance with France that could potentially reduce his financial dependence on Parliament. In September 1668, his cherished sister and confidante, Henriette – married to Louis XIV's brother Philippe – advised Charles that such an alliance 'would be the veritable foundation of your own greatness', offering access to French troops, who would be 'practically in sight of England, could keep it in check and render Parliament more amenable'. Once covert relations with the French court were underway, Charles provided Henriette with a cipher for future correspondence, warning that 'the whole matter [must] be an absolute secret, otherwise we shall never compass the end we aim at'.[34] Indeed, when Pepys caught wind of a rumour in April 1669 that private French financial subsidies might offer Charles a means of achieving independence from Parliament, he judged it 'a thing that will make the Parliament and kingdom mad, and will turn to our ruin'.[35]

Notwithstanding, Charles spent his fortieth birthday on 29 May 1670 – coinciding with the tenth anniversary of his restoration – at Dover, relishing a visit from Henriette, with the strategic purpose of her trip concealed by shared enjoyment of yacht races, an expedition to Canterbury, banquets and a ballet performance. Five days earlier, a treaty had been signed in secret at Dover by four English Catholic courtiers and the French ambassador to London, Charles Colbert de Croissy. This envisaged a combined

Anglo-French invasion of the Dutch Republic and committed Charles to professing his conversion to Catholicism, while Louis undertook to provide regular financial support and, if necessary, troops to assist Charles in re-establishing Catholicism in all his kingdoms. A 'sanitized' version of the treaty – with all clauses concerning Catholicism excised – was later signed at Westminster in December, pledging an Anglo-French attack against the Dutch. On 3 June, Henriette's departure to France was observed by Croissy, who reported to Louis XIV that he had 'never seen before so sorrowful a leave-taking, or known before how much royal personages could love one another'; indeed, it was widely acknowledged that Henriette had 'much more power over the king her brother than any other person in the world'.[36] But when Henriette suddenly died later that month, Charles was consumed by anguish and his interest in the more risky aspects of the treaty soon evaporated. The controversial clauses relating to Charles's public conversion and England's return to Catholicism were quietly disregarded, while Louis supplied lump sum payments of £160,000 in 1672 and £230,000 the following year.

Fortified by French funds, Charles deployed prerogative action in January 1672 by suspending repayment on the majority of outstanding loans in a 'Stop of the Exchequer' that released over £1.2 million. Observing that 'the sad experience of twelve years' had shown there to be 'very little fruit' in forcibly promoting religious conformity, Charles issued a Declaration of Indulgence in March which suspended all penal laws and permitted Protestant dissenters to obtain licences for public worship and Roman Catholics to worship privately at home, before declaring war on the Dutch two days later.[37] Military success proved elusive, however, and when the English Parliament next convened in February 1673, Charles could obtain further financial supply only by withdrawing the provisions of his Indulgence and reluctantly accepting a new 'Test Act' that prohibited anyone from holding public office who refused to deny the Catholic doctrine of transubstantiation. Clearly directed at Charles's brother and heir presumptive, the Duke of York, the Test Act's terms prompted York's resignation as Lord High Admiral in June, after his failure to take Anglican communion at Easter publicly confirmed his conversion to Catholicism. York's status as heir presumptive became increasingly significant with every year that passed in which no offspring were born to the king and queen, even though, by 1673, Charles had sired yet more illegitimate children: two sons, Charles (later Duke of St Albans) and James (Lord Beauclerk), by the actress Nell Gwyn; a son, Charles (later Duke of Richmond and Duke of Lennox), by Louise de Kérouaille (later Duchess of Portsmouth); and a daughter, Mary (later Countess of Derwentwater), by another actress, Mary ('Moll') Davis.

The rising tide of visceral anti-Catholicism swelled when the widowed Duke of York then married an Italian Catholic, Mary of Modena, in September 1673, thereby raising the spectre of a perpetual Catholic dynasty, should his new wife produce a son. Amid annual celebrations on 5 November that year, to commemorate the foiling of the

Gunpowder Plot, an effigy of the pope was carried in procession and publicly burned in London in what could plausibly be construed as satirical enactment of York's future coronation entry into the city. Charles's staunch support for his brother remained intact, however, and was observed the following year by the Venetian representative in London, Girolamo Alberti, who attended a dinner at which 'the king, throwing aside all reserve, tenderly embraced his brother several times, declaring that those who sought to separate them were rebels'. The 'tears of tenderness' accompanying Charles's outburst 'might have been attributed in others to weakness of head', mused Alberti, but no one present 'doubts the genuineness of the demonstration'.[38]

Fraternal solidarity did not, however, allay suspicions regarding the king's pro-French leanings and, by the mid 1670s, charged clouds of mistrust were massing over Charles's court as tensions increased between monarch and Parliament. In 1673, Charles appointed Sir Thomas Osborne (later Earl of Danby) as treasurer, who increased royal solvency by skilful management of crown revenue, boosted by an expansion in trade. Danby also tried to assuage anti-Catholic anxieties by visibly supporting the established Church and promoting a pro-Protestant foreign policy that included a popular decision by Charles to marry York's elder daughter, Mary, to the Dutch Stadholder, William of Orange, in 1677. Yet as Danby consolidated support for royal policy through an extensive patronage network of parliamentary placemen and one-off payments to secure loyalty, the court's retreat from religious inclusiveness in favour of a partisan endorsement of the Anglican establishment began to encourage disquieting parallels to be drawn between Charles's reign and that of his father. An anonymous *Letter from a Person of Quality* (1675) – often attributed to Anthony Ashley Cooper, Earl of Shaftesbury, and John Locke – identified 'a distinct party' that attracted 'the High Episcopal Man and the Old Cavalier' intent on seeking 'to fight the old quarrel over again' with their former adversaries, and regretted that Charles II lacked 'a temper robust, and laborious enough' to withstand such pressure.[39]

As the 'Cavalier Parliament' that had been elected in 1661 continued sitting without re-election, the erstwhile Parliamentarian leader Denzil Lord Holles complained in 1676 about its unrepresentative nature, since its members had been elected at a time 'when the people of England were in a kind of delirium or dotage'.[40] Theories of malevolent conspiracy were elaborated in Andrew Marvell's anonymously published *Account of the Growth of Popery and Arbitrary Government* (1677), which purported to accept that, although Charles 'would strip himself to his shirt rather than hazard the nation', he had become the victim of systematic intrigue to 'change the lawful government of England into an absolute tyranny' and to substitute Protestantism with 'downright popery'. Skilfully presenting radically subversive claims as ostensibly uncontroversial, Marvell insisted that 'as none will deny' that converting the monarchy into a republican commonwealth had been treasonable in the 1650s, 'so by the same fundamental rule, the crime is no less to make that monarchy absolute'.[41]

Royalists, however, distrusted such postures of disingenuous counsel from Charles's most trenchant critics. Identifying the 'crocodile of 41', the government's press licensor, Roger L'Estrange, grimly recalled civil war pamphlets which had proclaimed 'nothing but love and reverence to his late Majesty too, till his head was off'.[42]

As politics became increasingly polarized, Charles received 'revelations' in August 1678 via a clerical informer, Israel Tonge, and a renegade priest, Titus Oates, of an alleged Jesuitical plot to assassinate him, install his brother as king and return England to Catholicism. Despite Charles's cool assurance to Parliament that he would 'leave the matter to the law', some of his privy councillors and the general public quickly convinced themselves of the plot's veracity.[43] Critics of Charles's policies made capital from the rumoured conspiracy, fuelling fears that Jesuits had intended to set fire to London for a second time in a giant pro-Catholic conflagration. Circumstantial details added credibility to the alleged plot, especially after the magistrate to whom Oates had sworn his deposition, Sir Edmund Berry Godfrey, was found murdered and incriminating correspondence was discovered between Louis XIV's confessor and the Duke of York's former secretary. In response, Catholics were banned from London, searches for priests were conducted across the country and twenty Catholic laymen and thirteen priests were executed. In November, the House of Commons passed a motion calling for the queen and all Catholics to be removed from Whitehall, although the proposal was defeated in the Lords. The following month, however, documents were

produced in the Commons by Charles's former ambassador to France, Ralph Montagu, revealing that – for all his
outward rhetoric of a partisan pro-Protestant foreign
policy – Danby had simultaneously been involved in secret
negotiations with the French court for further subsidies
aimed at freeing Charles from financial dependence on
Parliament.

The political fallout from the 'Popish Plot' quickly
swelled into a full-blown 'Exclusion Crisis' when a bill
demanding that Charles's Catholic brother and heir, the
Duke of York, be removed from the royal line of succession
passed its second reading in the Commons by a majority of
seventy-nine votes in May 1679. Often identified as the
predicament that created modern Britain's two-party
political system, the Exclusion Crisis pitted Charles II and
his 'Tory' supporters against a 'Whig' opposition, led by
the Earl of Shaftesbury. While Tory loyalists insisted that
altering the hereditary succession after Charles's death
would return the country to the chaos of civil war, their
Whig opponents argued that the nation's Protestant establishment simply could not withstand the accession of a
Catholic monarch. Aside from the personal sadness arising from her infertility, Catherine of Braganza's inability
to provide Charles with an heir thus threatened to desta-
bilize the restored monarchy as the same anxieties that
had accompanied the 'succession crisis' during the reign
of Elizabeth I resurfaced. In practical terms, excluding
the king's brother meant either obliging Charles to
divorce Catherine and remarry, or legitimizing Charles's
eldest natural son, the Duke of Monmouth, who was

increasingly hailed as a popular, Protestant alternative to his Catholic uncle.

Persistent rumours of a clandestine, youthful marriage between Charles and Monmouth's mother, Lucy Walter, forced Charles to issue three separate declarations confirming that 'I never was married nor gave any contract to any woman whatsoever but to my wife, Queen Catherine, to whom I am now married'.[44] In August 1679, Charles removed both Monmouth and York from London – to the Netherlands and Scotland respectively – and issued seven successive prorogations to prevent Parliament reconvening between October 1679 and October 1680, thereby frustrating further legislative attempts at exclusion. Although, as a rule, Charles was a pragmatic and flexible political operator, maintaining hereditary succession as an integral part of the dignity of monarchical authority was the one principle over which he refused to compromise, precisely because he had himself been deprived of his thrones for over a decade after his father's execution. A second Exclusion Bill was defeated in the Lords in November 1680, and was followed by Parliament's dissolution. Following fresh elections, a new parliament convened in Oxford in March 1681, when Charles denounced attempts at exclusion as an illegal invasion of the royal prerogative, firmly insisting that 'I, who will never use arbitrary government myself, am resolved not to suffer it in others'.[45] Finding MPs still intent on pursuing exclusion, Charles dissolved the 'Oxford Parliament' after one week and never called an English parliament again.

Realizing that public opinion dreaded a descent into

1. In Van Dyck's *Three Eldest Children of Charles I* (1635), the five-year-old Prince Charles offers a reassuring arm to his young brother, James, who stands between Charles and his older sister, Mary. Following Charles I's execution in 1649, this poignant family portrait was sold to a Parliamentarian army officer before being acquired by Sir Peter Lely, who returned it to Charles II after the Restoration.

2. *Charles II Discovered by Colonel Careless and William Penderel Seated on a Tree-stump in Boscobel Wood* by Isaac Fuller (*c.*1660s) was one of five narrative canvases illustrating Charles's flight from the Battle of Worcester in 1651. Camouflaged in rustic clothing and sitting with his flies seemingly open, Charles's kingly status is indicated only by his companions' deferential poses.

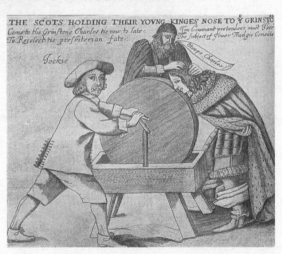

THE SCOTS HOLDING THEIR YOVNG KINGES NOSE TO Y GRINSTO

Come to the Grinstone Charles tie now to late
To Recolech his presbiterian fate.

You Counant pretenders must their
The subiect of your Tradgie Comedie

Jockie

Scrape Charles?

3. The broadside illustration *The Scots Holding their Young King's Nose to the Grindstone* (1651) satirized the stringent conditions exacted from Charles before his austere coronation at Scone Palace on 1 January 1650.

4. Hieronymus Janssens's *Charles II Dancing at a Ball at Court* (*c.*1660) is probably an imagined reconstruction of a banquet held in Charles's honour at The Hague, shortly before his return to England. In this painting, Charles appears twice: dancing in the outer room with his sister Mary, Princess of Orange, and dining in the inner room, seated next to Mary.

5 and 6. Two unfinished and undated miniatures of Charles II and his wife, Catherine of Braganza, by Samuel Cooper. Known to have been painted *ad vivum*, the likeness of Charles evinces a rare intimacy, while the painting of Queen Catherine dates from the time of the couple's marriage in 1662.

7. This painting of Barbara Villiers and Charles Fitzroy (*c*.1664) by Sir Peter Lely epitomizes the audacity with which baroque portraiture's conventional pieties were derailed when Charles II's court painter chose to present the king's favourite mistress and her son by Charles as the Madonna and Child.

8. Although Charles's amorous pursuit of Frances Stuart was unsuccessful, her figurative appearance as 'Britannia' in Jan Roettier's medal commemorating the Peace of Breda (1667) reflected this king's dangerous tendency to conflate private lust and state affairs.

9. Charles reportedly hung Sir Peter Lely's *Portrait of a Young Woman and Child, as Venus and Cupid* (*c*.1670s) – believed to be of another favoured mistress, Nell Gwyn – behind a landscape painting that could be swung back to allow private viewings.

10. Measuring nearly ten feet high, John Michael Wright's full-frontal *Charles II* is an iconic image of the restored Stuart monarchy, in which Charles wears the new version of St Edward's Crown made for his coronation in 1661.

11. *Charles II Presented with a Pineapple* (c.1675–80) is unusual in depicting the king in fashionable clothing from the 1670s rather than ceremonial attire.

The Royal Gift of Healing

12. Robert White's engraving of Charles II touching a patient for the king's evil (scrofula) appeared as the frontispiece to John Browne's treatise, *Adenochoiradelogia . . . or King's-Evil-swellings* (1684).

13. This flamboyant and over-life-sized bust of Charles II, with billowing drapery and tight ringlets, was sculpted in marble by the French artist Honoré Pellé in 1684.

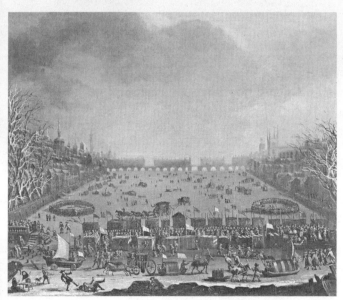

14. In January 1684, Charles and his family visited 'Freezeland', depicted here in *The Frost Fair of the Winter of 1683–4 on the Thames, with Old London Bridge in the Distance.*

15. Cedric Hardwicke and Anna Neagle as Charles II and Nell Gwyn in the film *Nell Gwyn* (1934), directed by Neagle's husband, Herbert Wilcox.

16. Undoubtedly a travesty of Charles II's actual physical appearance, the lascivious and cynical character portrayed in Thomas Hawker's *King Charles II* (*c.*1680) continues to shape this king's posthumous image and reputational afterlife.

anarchy even more than it feared a Catholic successor, Charles seized the political initiative by directing charges of irresponsible recklessness against his Whig enemies. In April 1681, he issued a public declaration – which he commanded be read aloud in all parish churches – attacking 'the restless malice of ill men who are labouring to poison our people, some out of fondness for their old beloved Commonwealth principles' and some from private jealousies and resentments.[46] In July, he convened a Scottish parliament under the direction of the Duke of York as High Commissioner. Having stated its intention 'to let [Charles's] other kingdoms and all the world see' the illegality of exclusion, the Scottish Parliament's Succession Act (1681) confirmed that monarchical succession was solely determined by proximity of blood and was unalterable by parliamentary statute.[47] Victory in the Exclusion Crisis thereafter unleashed a partisan 'Tory Reaction' that lasted for the rest of Charles's reign and attracted considerable popular support. Depicting his Whig adversaries as dangerous republican rebels, Charles's administration purged local commissions of the peace, remodelled municipal boroughs and interfered with judicial appointments. Further political capital was secured in June 1683 when another Whig-sponsored conspiracy, known as the 'Rye House Plot', was uncovered, with its intention to assassinate both Charles and York on their return from attending horse-racing at Newmarket. At the same time, annual crown revenue increased by more than a quarter from £1.1 million to £1.4 million, largely through fiscal levies on overseas trade. During his final years as king, Charles thus became, as his physician James Welwood put it, 'quite lulled asleep with the charms of a new-swelled up prerogative'.[48]

On 2 February 1685, however, Charles became critically ill, suffering either a stroke or the exacerbation of chronic kidney disease. He died four days later at Whitehall, having been received into the Catholic Church on his deathbed, at York's encouragement. By curiously fitting coincidence, the priest summoned to hear Charles's deathbed confession was Father John Huddleston, who, thirty-four years earlier, had courageously sheltered Charles during his dramatic flight from Worcester. Although a state funeral had initially been planned, a scaled-down evening burial was held, reflecting the nervousness that surrounded his brother's accession as the first openly Catholic monarch of England since the unfortunate reign of Mary Tudor. Although Charles had been seriously ill in 1679 and 1682, his death came as a shock. Only a week earlier, Evelyn recalled observing 'a scene of utmost vanity' at court, comprising 'the King, sitting and toying with his concubines . . . a French boy singing love songs in that glorious gallery' and about 'twenty of the great courtiers and other dissolute persons' gambling large sums at cards. As Evelyn mused, those present 'thought they would never have an end: six days after was all in the dust'.[49]

3
Image

In physical appearance, Charles II cut a distinctive figure and, even today, his image is easily recognized by many who otherwise know little about the seventeenth century. A large, swarthy baby, he was described by his mother as 'so fat and tall' at four months 'that he [was] taken for a year old', though she admitted 'he is so dark that I am ashamed of him'.[1] As an adult, Charles grew to six feet two inches, which meant that he towered over most contemporaries and offered a stark contrast to his father, Charles I, who had stood at only five feet four inches. In portraits, Charles often chose to be depicted in his Garter robes, which added another foot to his height via a bonnet of white ostrich plumes and black heron feathers. His unusual height and olive complexion had, however, proved a potential liability when he donned various disguises to escape his Parliamentarian enemies in 1651, and he later wryly recalled chatting to a domestic servant near Bristol, who had formerly served in his own regiment and who innocently described the king as being 'at least three fingers taller than I'.[2] In exile, Charles grew the slender pencil moustache that he retained until 1677 and always sedulously maintained his appearance: the royal barber,

Monsieur Folliart, used only 'the freshest whipped egg-white for shaving his master and applied scented essence, powder and pomade afterwards'.[3]

At the Restoration, there was a particularly urgent need to familiarize subjects with their new king's physical appearance, since Charles had not resided permanently in England since he was a teenager and displaying images of the 'King of Scots' had been made a criminal offence during the republican Commonwealth. Shortly before Charles's return from the continent, one London correspondent wrote to Edward Hyde, describing popular anticipation and recounting how Charles's 'picture is hung up in many places in the streets'. Indeed, the writer had overheard one passer-by object that, having recently seen the king in exile, 'he was not so handsome as that picture, at which the people were so angry that they fell upon the man and beat him soundly'.[4] With Charles deliberately trying to ensure that his image was as widely disseminated as possible, depictions of him quickly appeared in numerous prints, as well as on objects, from dishes, mugs, tankards and wine bottles to tiles and jewellery. Acquiring items bearing the new king's portrait was a clear way of confirming loyalty to the new regime, although the Royalist Roger L'Estrange scorned such ostentation as patent opportunism. As he observed of Charles's newest supporters, 'Out comes the spruce tobacco-box, with the king's picture at it, which he wears, and kisses . . . as for a hint, and introduction, to his politics, now at hand.'[5]

Most images of the new king were also outdated. During the 1650s, numerous engravings of a portrait by the

Dutch artist Adriaen Hanneman had been produced, showing Charles aged eighteen, shortly before his father's execution, wearing a buff military coat and breastplate. Charles could not, however, be painted wearing a crown while in exile, for despite having been crowned King of Scotland in 1651, the royal regalia had remained in Scotland. Instead, the exiled court commissioned images of Charles in armour or wearing other regalia, such as the Order of the Garter, to sustain Royalist loyalties and confirm his authority. To compensate for the lack of an accurate visual likeness, sundry authors instead produced 'pen portraits' of the king for his new subjects. A former Royalist officer who had joined the exiled court, Sir Samuel Tuke, described the king's hair, for example, as being 'of a shining black, not frizzied, but so naturally curling into great rings, that it is a very comely ornament'. Tuke acknowledged that Charles's complexion was 'somewhat dark, but much enlightened by his eyes which are quick and sparkling'.[6] Basing his *Heroic Portraits* (1660) on observations of the exiled court in Brussels, the poet Richard Flecknoe described Charles in similar terms:

> His visage oval, his hair thick and black,
> In ample curls, on his shoulders falling down,
> Adorning his head, [more] than any crown.[7]

Even the most sensuous descriptions of Charles's external appearance nevertheless also tended to acknowledge a steelier persona within. In his posthumous character sketch of the king, the Marquis of Halifax claimed that 'those who knew his face, fixed their eyes there', deeming it more important to watch the king's expression than listen to his words, acknowledging that Charles's facial expressions 'would sometimes tell tales to a good observer'. Indeed, Halifax justified including ostensibly negative character traits in his account as equivalent to instances in portraiture when 'some rough strokes of the pencil have made several parts of the picture look a little hard'.[8] Attending Charles's court in the 1660s, a young Italian diplomat, Lorenzo Magalotti, likewise identified 'a certain smiling look' from the king that 'so greatly clears and softens the roughness of his features'.[9] More specifically, Charles was often likened in appearance to the emperor Tiberius; reminiscing later, even his physician, James Welwood, concurred that 'in the lines and shape of his face' the king had resembled busts and statues of the reclusive Roman ruler.[10]

Ironically for a monarch whose image became so widely available, very few portraits of Charles were painted from life – or *ad vivum* – with a small number of actual sittings providing prototypes for extensive duplication and elaboration. Among the most accurate likenesses to survive are four *ad vivum* studies undertaken by the miniaturist Samuel Cooper soon after the Restoration (see picture 5). Now at Chiddingstone Castle in Kent, one of Cooper's unfinished portraits clearly shows Charles's laughter lines, with the king's eyelids and eyelashes deftly silhouetted alongside his lustrous dark hair. Whereas a formal state portrait had accompanied every new English monarch's accession since Henry VIII, the fact that no official commission was undertaken in 1660 reflected the precariousness attaching to Charles's position. The earliest known representation of the restored monarch was instead John Michael Wright's *Astraea*, which had been hung from the ceiling of the royal bedroom at Whitehall by 1662 and included a medallion portrait of Charles being borne skywards by putti, while cupids were depicted supporting the Boscobel Oak. It was also shortly after Charles's coronation in April 1661 that Wright is thought to have painted one of the Restoration's most iconic images, and which remains in the Royal Collection: a full-length frontal portrait, nearly ten feet high, of Charles in coronation robes, seated under a canopy of state, wearing the newly fashioned St Edward's Crown, and holding the royal orb and sceptre (see picture 10). The portrait also included a Latin verse from the Book of Chronicles to describe how 'Solomon sat on the throne of the Lord as king instead of David his father and prospered; and all Israel obeyed him'.[11]

The majority of portraits, however, avoided overt claims to Charles's divinely ordained status, preferring to depict the king in his Garter robes, of which the scarlet surcoat, indigo lining, silver ribbons and delicate lace supplied a striking display and evoked comfortably nostalgic Tudor memories. As more 'transactional' approaches to portraiture gained popularity in the late seventeenth century, painters increasingly eschewed the aim of producing a 'true' likeness, endowing their subjects instead with visual personae that could be appreciated by both contemporaries and posterity. In this vein, one audacious example of visual propaganda was *The Sea Triumph of Charles II* by the Italian artist Antonio Verrio, which is thought to have been painted shortly after the Dutch had effectively conceded supremacy of the seas to the English by the Treaty of Westminster (1674). Now at Hampton Court Palace, Verrio's painting depicts Charles in classical armour, being steered through the sea in a shell-like chariot by Neptune, with a troop of white horses and three female figures bearing the triple crowns of England, Scotland and Ireland. Even more ostentatious was a pictorial panegyric – destroyed by fire in the early nineteenth century – that Verrio created for the redesigned royal apartments at Windsor Castle, which included an image for the Presence Chamber of the Roman god Mercury presenting Charles's portrait to the four corners of the earth. Verrio also produced the painting *Christ Healing the Sick at Capernaum* for the chapel at Windsor, thereby offering implicit homage to Charles, who – as the next chapter relates – undertook more 'royal healing' in emulation of Christ than any other monarch in British history. In the aftermath of the Exclusion Crisis, Charles commissioned the Dutch painter Jacob de Wet to paint portraits of his 111 putative Stuart ancestors to hang in Holyrood Palace in Edinburgh, a selection of which still hangs there today. These images thus provided powerful pictorial confirmation of the Scottish Parliament's recent Succession Act (1681), which had firmly condemned as treasonable any attempts to alter the hereditary line to the throne after Charles's death.

In the early years of the Restoration, Charles's civil war experiences nevertheless posed a challenge for portraitists. As one modern critic has put it: 'how does an artist depict a king who had successfully disguised himself as a peas-ant?'[12] Isaac Fuller's response was to produce five canvases, each seven feet high and up to ten feet wide, that supplied a narrative account of Charles's flight from the Battle of Worcester. Perhaps initially commissioned as an interior decoration scheme and now owned by the National Por-trait Gallery, Fuller's paintings of Charles's experiences on the run portray the king as indistinguishable in appear-ance from his humblest subjects (see picture 2). His vignettes include undignified depictions of the king sitting casually, seemingly unaware that his flies remain undone; perched awkwardly on an aged mill-horse; and asleep in the Bosco-bel Oak. In another commemorative painting celebrating Charles's escape from Worcester, the royal Serjeant Painter, Robert Streeter, produced a huge representation of Bosco-bel House, and the nearby lodging Whiteladies, with numbers painted on the canvas to lead viewers sequentially through Charles's dramatic flight.

Once restored as king, however, Charles evidently had little patience for portrait sittings. When asked by his brother the Duke of York to sit for a likeness by the Dutch painter Peter Lely, and by his son the Duke of Monmouth to sit for another by the Lübeck-born painter Godfrey Kneller, the king's suggestion that both should paint him simultaneously resulted in a competitive 'trial of skill' in 1677 or 1678. In an account written in the 1720s by the engraver George Vertue, Lely is described sketching out his portrait for subsequent finishing, while his ambitious younger rival, Kneller, being 'full of fire and ambition', tri-umphed by both drawing and painting Charles's portrait and was 'seemingly finished at once'. Charles could also be disconcertingly self-deprecating about his appearance, and reportedly devastated the royal portraitist, John Riley, by examining a finished likeness and exclaiming 'Is this like me? Odd's Fish, then I'm an ugly fellow!'[13] Nevertheless, since most depictions of Charles derive from a very limited number of actual sittings, it is ironic that perhaps the best-known image today of Charles II remains a portrait by Thomas Hawker – on display in the National Portrait Gallery – that is very unlikely to have been painted from life (see picture 16). Exuding an unmistakably lascivious mien, the king's face is careworn and middle-aged, but his hands are visibly younger; his head was evidently modelled on a previous portrait by Riley, the pose taken from another image by Kneller and the flounced clothing echoing Wright's earlier paintings.

The polemical potential of art could thus be equally as effective in undermining monarchy as in venerating royal power. During the 1650s, Charles had endured the circulation of satirically humiliating – if depressingly accurate – cartoons satirizing his subjugation by Scottish Presbyterians, bearing such titles as *The Scots Holding their Young King's Nose to the Grindstone* (see picture 3). Once Charles has been restored to his rightful thrones, the need to promote images of him as widely as possible inevitably compromised their quality and execution, prompting observers such as John Evelyn to express horror at seeing Charles's likeness ubiquitously exploited on rustic 'signs, among cats, owls, dogs and asses, at the pleasure of every tavern and tippling-house'.[14] In 1672, the Venetian Girolamo

Alberti likewise denounced 'the unbearable effrontery of the Dutch', who felt themselves 'at liberty to abuse all sovereigns' and whose burgeoning print market spawned numerous derogatory images, including ones that showed 'his Britannic Majesty with a ring through his nose' being 'led by the King of France'.[15] Indeed, in his official declaration of war against the Dutch that year, Charles identified 'abusive pictures' and 'false historical medals' as a specific provocation, while *A Justification of the Present War* (1672) by the physician Henry Stubbe similarly deplored Dutch malice in 'rendering the English cheap and ridiculous by their lying pictures, and libelling pamphlets'. As Stubbe warned, cartoons depicting the English monarch as a lion with cropped ears or a dog with a docked tail 'take much with the barbarous people' unless officially suppressed.[16]

As politics became increasingly partisan in the early 1680s, one of the most trenchant pictorial attacks on royal power came in the form of an illustrated poem entitled *The Raree Show* (1681). On one side, it depicted a two-faced Charles (half Protestant, half papist) as a travelling pedlar, carrying a portable peep-show – the Houses of Parliament – from city to city, while one of Charles's two faces blew bubbles, denoting the emptiness of royal words. On the other side, the royal pedlar is shown stuck in mire, having reached Oxford from London, with trapped MPs escaping from his pack. The deadly consequences of association with such a pointed graphic attack on Charles's handling of the Oxford Parliament became clear in court, however, when the crown's lawyers denounced a radical

Exclusionist, Stephen College, for 'publishing libels, and pictures to make the king odious and contemptible in the eyes of the people'.[17] Convicted of treason, College was executed in August 1681, despite denying responsibility for the poem's authorship, illustration or publication.

Offence could, however, equally be generated by paintings emanating from the royal court itself. A representational portrait of Queen Catherine as St Catherine of Alexandria by the Flemish artist Jacob Huysman, for example, self-consciously sought to endow the queen with some of the saint's qualities, such as beauty, fearlessness and intelligence. More commonly during the Restoration, however, sacral images of monarchy were inverted and religious references mocked. Derailing the conventionally virtuous symbolism of baroque portraiture, Lely adopted Charles's mistress the Countess of Castlemaine as his chief muse and variously portrayed her as Minerva, Roman goddess of wisdom, Pallas, the spear-bearing Greek goddess of wisdom and courage, and, most shockingly, with one of her sons by Charles II as a Madonna and Child (see picture 7). Hanging today in the National Portrait Gallery, this portrait, with its depiction of Castlemaine's loose red and blue robes, echoes traditional portrayals of the Virgin and not all viewers would necessarily have appreciated its satirical implications. As the connoisseur Horace Walpole later recounted, Castlemaine even sent a version of Lely's quasi-blasphemous image of the 'Madonna and little Jesus' to a French convent, where it served as an altar-piece for several years before 'the nuns, discovering whose portrait it was, returned it'.[18]

More generally, Lely's erotic evocations of female beauty – the diaphanous clothing, languorous poses and allegorical subject matter – epitomized the sensual excesses that characterized the Restoration court. The shocking example supplied by Charles's 'painted ladies' and foppishly attired male associates provoked predictable Puritan outrage. The theologian Richard Baxter, for instance, used his preface to the English translation of Jacques Boileau's *A Just and Seasonable Reprehension of Naked Breasts and Shoulders* (1678) to lament the 'general tawdry in London', 'vanity of fashion' and 'monstrous periwigs'. Invoking God's recent judgements of plague and fire, Baxter urged readers to recall 'what a sight London was in ruins' and how 'carcasses of men and women were heaped upon one another in pits'.[19] Undeterred, attendants at Charles's court, male and female alike, continued to embrace flamboyant French fashions, such as a 'flat foam of lace' around the shoulders and chest, but as foreign policy officially turned against France in the mid 1670s, Charles declared that he would 'henceforth wear none but English manufactures except linen and calico' and ordered all his subjects likewise to desist from foreign attire amid public burnings of French hats and gloves.[20]

More permanent commemoration of Charles – and a simultaneous means of promoting royal authority – could be achieved by commissioning statues. After the Great Fire, full-length statues of Charles and his father and grandfather were created by John Bushnell for Temple Bar in the City of London. The statues presented the monarchs in classical attire, albeit sporting seventeenth-century moustaches, beards, long hair, Garter insignia and royal crowns. On Charles's forty-second birthday in May 1672, an equestrian statue was unveiled at Stocks Market, also in the City. Imported from Italy, the unfinished statue had originally been intended to depict one of the victories of the Polish king John III Sobieski over the Ottoman Turks, but an unknown sculptor then converted the mangled statue – now at Newby Hall in Yorkshire – into an image of Charles trampling on a turbaned Oliver Cromwell. Three years later, an equestrian statue of Charles I, by the French sculptor Hubert Le Sueur, was erected in Charing Cross – where it remains today – directly surveying the site of the former king's execution outside the Banqueting House. The close proximity to each other of these two statues provided irresistible temptation to satirists disillusioned by Charles's administration. In 'A Dialogue between the Two Horses' (1676), attributed to Marvell, the two animals anthropomorphically rued their respective masters' shortcomings: the Charing Cross horse explained that his master was consulting with 'Bishop Laud' while the Stocks Market steed admitted that the younger Charles was currently in disguise, cuckolding a scrivener, before exclaiming, 'A Tudor! A Tudor! We've had Stuarts enough; / None ever reigned like Old Bess in the ruff!'[21]

On a grander scale, in 1679 the sculptor Grinling Gibbons executed an oversized bronze equestrian statue of Charles in classical costume which was commissioned to stand in the grounds of Windsor Castle in an artistic statement that pre-dated anything similar commemorating Louis XIV of France, with whom such grandiose statuary is more often associated. Shortly after Charles's death, a replica of Gibbons's statue was unveiled in Parliament Square in Edinburgh – where it still stands today – at which the lawyer Sir John Lauder of Fountainhall reported that 'the vulgar people, who had never seen the like before, were much amazed at it'. Interpreting the statue in biblical terms, some compared it to 'Nebuchadnezzar's image, which all fell down and worshipped', while others likened it 'foolishly to the pale horse in the Revelation', fearing 'he that sat thereon was Death'.[22] Other three-dimensional images included Bushnell's terracotta bust of Charles, with intricately sculpted wig and cravat, now in Cambridge's Fitzwilliam Museum, and an elaborately detailed, larger-than-life marble bust of the king by the French sculptor Honoré Pellé, which can be seen today in the Victoria and Albert Museum (see picture 13).[23]

The most enduring way to confirm the permanence of the restored monarchy was, however, through civic architecture. Following years of civil war, regicide and republicanism, representing monarchical authority in Portland stone conveyed a sense of physical durability and political stability. As the speculative builder Nicholas Barbon commented in 1685: 'Every man that builds a house, gives security to the government for his good behaviour.'[24] Furthermore, Charles II was uniquely well placed to oversee such rebuilding: during more than a decade in exile on the continent, he had observed more royal palaces and grandiose civic architecture abroad than any of his predecessors. Following the re-establishment of the king's Office of Works, ambitious plans were therefore devised to restore

and redesign the royal palaces, including a radical reconstruction of Whitehall Palace, together with the creation of
a new palace at Greenwich to provide 'the ceremonial gate-
way to his kingdom' where monarchs could receive foreign
envoys and dignitaries before accompanying them upriver
to London.[25] Writing in 1664, John Evelyn commended
Charles for having effected more new building in the first
few years of his reign than his enemies had destroyed in the
previous two decades, citing new paving in Westminster
Hall, renovations at St Paul's Cathedral and improvements
and enlargements to the Queen Mother's apartments at
Somerset House.[26] Hence even before the rebuilding that
followed the Great Fire, Charles was being compared by
the architect John Webb to the Roman emperor Augustus,
who left 'Rome a city of marble, [having found it] ignobly
built', insisting that 'no Prince, now living, understands a
drawing more knowingly'.[27]

Reproduced images of Charles II's residences also
inspired interior decoration schemes among loyal supporters, such as Pepys, who in 1669 commissioned depictions
of Whitehall, Hampton Court, Greenwich and Windsor
by the Dutch painter Hendrick Danckerts to hang in his
dining room before randomly substituting a painting of
Rome for that of Hampton Court two months later. That
same year, Charles appointed Christopher Wren, then
Savilian Professor of Astronomy at Oxford, as Surveyor of
the King's Works in a post that would assure the reign's
architectural legacy through an enduring transformation
of London's physical appearance. Although Wren's tenure
as surveyor until 1718 lasted longer than the Stuart

monarchy, Wren's son later claimed that his father had 'been often heard to complain . . . that King Charles II had done him a disservice in . . . obliging him to spend all his time in rubbish (the expression he had for building)' instead of allowing him to focus on his scientific studies and explore the more lucrative opportunities available in medicine.[28]

For in September 1666, the Great Fire had provided an unexpected opportunity to consider rebuilding London to a degree that would reflect monarchical munificence on a grandiose scale. Seeking to impose an elegant new coherence upon the English capital, Charles could thereby assume the role of the nation's architect, restoring London not only literally after the physical destruction of the Fire, but metaphorically following the political ruination of the 1640s and 1650s. As the City still smouldered, Wren presented Charles with his vision for a new city on 10 September and rival plans were also proposed, in quick succession, by other Fellows of the Royal Society, including John Evelyn, Robert Hooke and William Petty. For Evelyn, the Fire offered a unique opportunity to create a new metropolis that would be 'fitter for commerce, apter for government, sweeter for health, [and] more glorious for beauty'.[29] Although a less ambitious rebuilding scheme was eventually adopted, Pepys was impressed to see 'the King with his kettledrums and trumpets' laying the foundation stone of the Royal Exchange in October 1667, while his brother the Duke of York added a Doric column a week later, and his cousin Prince Rupert another column a fortnight afterwards.[30] In the 1670s, Wren's Monument to the Fire offered Londoners an exciting new bird's-eye perspective of the City, although initial plans to include a bronze statue of Charles at its pinnacle were set aside amid fears that the government's detractors might thereby be tempted to liken Charles to the classical emperor Nero, who had deliberately set fire to ancient Rome in order to rebuild a new city in his own glory.

During the 1670s, Charles abandoned his ambitious vision for a new palace at Greenwich to concentrate on remodelling the royal apartments at Whitehall, as well as refurbishing and expanding Windsor Castle – unique among royal palaces in also serving as a military fortress – which he aimed to transform into his principal royal residence. Coinciding with a new royal practice of establishing a summer residency at Windsor, the building works at the castle created new apartments for the king and queen and Duke and Duchess of York and a new chapel, while St George's Hall was entirely rebuilt. Retaining the Norman and medieval towers to emphasize historical continuity, as well as Henry VIII's Tower and Queen Elizabeth's Gallery, Charles added his 'Star Building' with its luminous façade of Portland stone to evoke the bright noon-day star that had shone so auspiciously at his birth. On the ceiling of St George's Hall an elaborate Garter Star and portrait of Charles II in Garter robes were installed, while internal wood carvings of roses, thistles, harps and crowns – no longer surviving – reminded viewers of the triple-crowned nature of the Stuart inheritance.

In the aftermath of the Exclusion Crisis, Charles

embarked on his most ambitious architectural project to date: planning the construction of a royal residence that, if completed, would have been the first new palace to be built from scratch by an English monarch since Henry VIII. The chosen location was an elevated site overlooking the city of Winchester, which not only offered welcome rural respite from febrile London politics, but also returned the royal court to Alfred the Great's ancient monarchical seat. Neglected after the king's death in 1685, Winchester Palace was never completed, but plans drawn up by Wren included a full suite of state apartments for Charles, Catherine and the Duke and Duchess of York, together with accommodation for official meetings, including secretarial offices and a council chamber. Symmetrical in design with state apartments radiating out from a central hallway and peacefully set within a spacious hunting park, Winchester Palace would have been Charles II's Versailles.

One of the last architectural 'innovations' of Charles's reign was the 'Frost Fair' that sprung up spontaneously when the River Thames froze solid between December 1683 and February 1684 (see picture 14). Dubbed 'Freezeland' by contemporaries, and situated in an area upriver of London Bridge, it consisted of so many speedily erected booths and taverns that they formed whole streets, with horse-drawn coaches regularly plying back and forth across the river, while Charles himself commissioned a detailed map to record the temporary new city's physical layout. Together with his wife, brother York and two nieces, Mary and Anne, Charles visited the Frost Fair on 31 January 1684, went fox-hunting on the ice and obtained personalized souvenir tickets from a printing press.[31] Characteristically informal, with street-vendors and printers evading official scrutiny, the carnivalesque fun of the Frost Fair – together with the inherently fragile foundation on which it was erected – offered an appropriate metaphor for Charles's reign.

4
Majesty

As an eight-year-old, Charles had learned about the impressive majesty of monarchical power from his mentor, the Earl of Newcastle, who had counselled the young prince that 'you cannot put upon you too much king'. Emphasizing the importance of ceremony – the whole panoply of fine furniture, rich attire, ornate coaches and heralds and trumpeters at court – Newcastle defined it as 'the mist [that] is cast before' all subjects.[1] At Charles's restoration, another author, James Heath, likewise advised the new king that his best strategy was to use 'State Grandezzas' to exploit the 'silent yet awful majesty' of 'magnificent public appearances'.[2] Given his early schooling in the vital importance of spectacle and ceremony in sustaining royal power, we should therefore be wary of accepting at face value Charles's derision of the Spanish Habsburg court when he objected to Pepys that his namesake Carlos II 'does nothing but under some ridiculous form or other, and will not piss but another must hold the chamber-pot'.[3] While Charles did not require a servant to hold his own chamber-pot, he was overlooking somewhat similar rituals at Whitehall: as a young courtier, Thomas Bruce, Earl of Ailesbury, recalled being required to hold a candle as the king relieved himself, while another groom 'who always had some amusing buffoonery in his head . . . held some paper'.[4]

Yet one of the most striking paradoxes about Charles was that, despite promoting a majestic image, reinforced by regular ritual, he was also one of British history's most accessible monarchs, combining the natural informality of his grandfather James I and VI with an innate gregariousness and personal magnetism. As king, he practised other sound advice he had received from Newcastle as a child, recognizing that sometimes doffing 'a hat or a smile in the right place will advantage you'.[5] Having also experienced at first hand the hardships of civil warfare and years of impecunious foreign exile, Charles had acquired rare royal insight into the lives of many of his subjects, as illustrated by his success in concealing his identity and evading capture during his legendary escape from Worcester in 1651, when he had adopted various disguises, from farm labourer to lady's manservant. Returning with the king from the Netherlands in 1660, Pepys recorded how one of Charles's favoured dogs '[shat] in the boat, which made us laugh', prompting the twenty-seven-year-old diarist to acknowledge 'that a King and all that belong to him are but just as others are'. The following year, Pepys confirmed that Charles's preferred attire was 'a plain common riding-suit and velvet cap', ensuring that 'he seemed a very ordinary man to one that had not known him'.[6] At Whitehall, Charles enjoyed strolling around and meeting people in the newly redesigned gardens in St James's Park that included a canal, ornamental waterworks and an aviary.

The actor and playwright Colley Cibber later recalled Charles's 'indolent amusement of playing with his dogs, and feeding his ducks in St James's Park', recognizing that the king's approachable demeanour 'made the common people adore him' and overlook other shortcomings in his personality.[7]

Whereas Charles I had preferred the privacy of Whitehall's confines, his son frequented plays in public theatres and attended civic entertainments, such as the Lord Mayor's Show in London. Away from the capital, Charles became particularly relaxed at Newmarket where, as the MP Sir John Reresby observed, he relished the various attractions so much 'that he let himself down from majesty to the very degree of a country gentleman', 'mixed himself among the crowd' and 'allowed every man to speak to him that pleased'.[8] On other occasions, the king's instinctive spontaneity even tested civic etiquette. Having sailed to Portsmouth in July 1671, for instance, Charles decided on a whim to sail onwards to Plymouth, where the local dignitaries were not only 'so surprised' by his sudden appearance in the town but, deprived of a chance to bid a formal farewell, they also 'went after him in a wherry' along the coast to the king's next destination, Mount Edgcumbe.[9]

In London, Charles primarily resided at Whitehall Palace, which initially extended to a chaotic maze of around 1,400 rooms for the royal family and courtiers. With large formal halls, chambers and countless corridors and secret stairways, the palace's architecture has been described as 'admirably suited to Charles's style of kingship, at once very open and devious'.[10] While Charles quickly sought to remodel and improve the outdated accommodation, boundaries between public and private spheres became increasingly blurred as he imported new practices from the continent, such as morning and evening rituals of 'lever' and 'coucher', whereby the king's daily dressing, shaving, donning his wig and preparing for bed were attended by courtiers and invited guests. Yet even by the early 1680s, Charles's court was never fastidious or austere. Ailesbury later recalled discomforts he had endured as a young courtier berthed in close proximity to the king to keep watch on 'Scotch coal' burning in smoky fires while 'a dozen dogs . . . came to our beds' and various clocks struck every fifteen minutes, but 'all not going alike, it was a continual chiming'.[11]

In a country that regarded ceremonial and communal eating as an accurate indicator of social status, Charles also revived the royal practice of dining in public, both at the Banqueting House and in his Presence Chamber. In doing so, he retained the emphasis on formal dining that had been maintained throughout his exile, despite reduced circumstances, when refined culinary standards survived fears of imminent bankruptcy or malnourishment. When the royal court was located in Paris in the summer of 1653, for example, Edward Hyde admitted that 'all of us owe for God knows how many weeks to the poor woman that feeds us'.[12] Privation nevertheless remained relative. While based in Cologne, for instance, the exiled court's lunch on 5 November 1655 comprised a veritable feast of roast chicken and partridge, veal, stewed quinces and fruit, while supper consisted of roast mutton with gravy, pigeon, lark and crayfish, with stewed apples and fruit for dessert.[13]

Unlike his Stuart predecessors, Charles received official deputations in his bedchamber and receptions for foreign ambassadors were as grand as the glittering state banquets laid on for foreign heads of state visiting Britain today. Seventeenth-century diplomatic protocol dictated the lavish exchange of presents, ensuring that in 1660, for example, Charles received a magnificent array of gifts, from Dutch fine art, furniture and sculpture, Russian sable and ermine furs and Venetian gondolas to live lions and ostriches from Morocco.[14] Keen to confirm their support for the restored monarchy, foreign diplomats also organized elaborate firework displays, sumptuous parties and paid for wine to flow in urban conduits. In striking contrast to the sombre mood of Charles I's execution a generation earlier, so many enthusiastic spectators filled the Banqueting House's upper balcony to observe a royal audience with the Russian ambassador in December 1662 that Pepys feared it might crash down under their gathered weight. Marvelling at the gifts of 'rich furs, hawks, carpets, cloths of tissue, and sea-horse teeth', Pepys watched Charles handle several hawks, his hand protected by a special glove 'wrought with gold'.[15]

To enhance the drama of his restoration, Charles had deliberately delayed his royal entry into London as king until his thirtieth birthday on 29 May 1660. The elaborate procession started in Deptford and passed through St George's Fields in Southwark before moving through the

City and Westminster, where Charles was presented with the sword of the City by the Lord Mayor, Sir Thomas Allen. Symbolic of the City's ancient liberties and independence from the crown, the sword was magnanimously returned by Charles to the Lord Mayor, who was then permitted to precede Charles in the ensuing procession. As well as numerous civic entertainments that summer, the City of London's livery companies also produced a spectacular aquatic pageant two years later, in August 1662, to mark Charles's marriage to Catherine of Braganza, which compensated for the absence of court-sponsored celebration. Evelyn was enraptured, deeming the display 'the most magnificent triumph that certainly ever floated on the Thames' and far superior to 'all the Venetian bucentaurs [state barges] on Ascension' Day, when the Doge would famously marry Venice to the sea. In August 1674, Charles organized a martial re-enactment at Windsor of the siege of Maastricht that required the construction of an extensive fort, moat and counterscarp. With around five hundred actors and volunteers serving as 'soldiers' in a defensive garrison, another seven hundred 'troops' attacked the castle, jointly commanded by the Dukes of York and Monmouth. While the latter had earned commendation for his conduct during the actual siege in June 1673, Charles's re-enactment ironically proved one of the last times that his brother and eldest son would co-operate, before becoming fatally estranged over attempts to exclude York from the royal succession. Having witnessed the spectacle with Pepys, Evelyn judged the reconstruction 'really most diverting', since it had appeared a convincing siege and 'all without disorder or ill accident, but to the great satisfaction of a thousand spectators'.[16]

The most magnificent ceremonial occasion of the reign was, however, Charles's coronation at Westminster Abbey on 23 April 1661, which included the crucial sacral element that confirmed his status as an individual chosen especially by God to rule. No previous monarch had been crowned on St George's Day before and, by choosing this date, Charles ensured that the two events would thereafter be celebrated simultaneously. He also insisted that the organizing committee consult archival records to make sure that his coronation conformed to ancient practice, thereby reinforcing the legitimacy of his accession. Having witnessed the lavish outdoor spectacle – also funded by the City of London's livery companies – that preceded the service, an exhausted Pepys concluded that he need never attend any future displays of 'state and show', being certain 'never to see the like again in this world', before waking the next day with a painful hangover.[17] The ceremonial theme had been devised by a Scottish impresario, John Ogilby, who presented Charles in heroic vein, both as Aeneas founding Rome following the fall of Troy and as the emperor Augustus, who had presided over the Roman Empire's most sustained era of peace and prosperity after republican turmoil. There were ample opportunities for spectators to see Charles – who had ordered five suits from Paris for the occasion – while provision of a maypole and Morris dancers indicated that the monarchy's return would be accompanied by the revival of popular pastimes after a decade of Puritan proscription.

Entertainment aside, the purpose of the occasion was critical to re-establishing princely power. The solemn symbiosis between restored monarchy and the established Church was confirmed when Charles swore the coronation oath, was anointed with holy oil and invested with the royal robes and regalia. In marked contrast to his Scottish coronation in 1651, where Charles had been humiliatingly reminded of his family's sins and obliged to seek public forgiveness, in the sermon preached at Westminster Abbey a decade later, Bishop George Morley of Worcester drew parallels between Charles and Christ as each sought to rebuild their respective kingdoms. A new set of Crown Jewels was also required for the coronation after their predecessors had been dismantled and melted down after the regicide. Although many of Charles I's belongings – paintings, statues, tapestries and other goods – had been sequestrated and sold following his execution, the Commonwealth regime recognized the importance of ensuring that the Crown Jewels could not be reconstituted and acquired by the exiled court. In 1661, however, the king's goldsmith, Robert Vyner, produced such exact replicas that an official guide to the Crown Jewels in the early eighteenth century could assert with confidence that the crown displayed in the Tower of London was that 'which all the kings of England have been crowned with, ever since Edward the Confessor's time'.[18]

Parallels between Charles and Christ extended to the way in which his subjects regarded the king as a sanctified physician who could cure his subjects' physical and spiritual ills. Indeed, no attribute underscored the quasi-divine character of English and French monarchs more than the purported gift of 'touching for the king's evil' – as a means of curing scrofula – and Charles's enthusiastic performance of this thaumaturgical ceremony confirmed the importance he attached to its role in maintaining royal authority (see picture 12). Although the royal touch was regarded by contemporaries as an effective cure for the painful and disfiguring glandular condition, the tendency for scrofula to flare up intermittently meant that receiving the royal touch could easily coincide with natural periods of remission. Between his restoration in 1660 and his death twenty-five years later, Charles touched around a hundred thousand individuals. In a published account of the royal touch – revealingly entitled *Charisma Basilicon* – one of Charles's surgeons, John Browne, appended official monthly figures confirming the number of people touched by the king. Charles had also continued the tradition in exile; as Browne recalled, a Scots merchant had 'made it his business every spring and fall to bring people from Scotland and Newcastle, troubled with the Evil, to the king where ever he was in his troubles'.[19] The ceremony itself involved a sick person kneeling before the king as a royal chaplain read aloud from the Bible, describing Christ's appearance after he had risen from the dead, with his message to the Apostles: 'They shall lay their hands on the sick and they shall recover.'[20] Each time this verse was read out, the king stroked the scrofula sufferer under the chin with both hands, before the sick person was presented again to the king, and given a commemorative 'touch-piece'.

Eminent foreign dignitaries were also invited to watch

'touching' ceremonies, albeit positioned tangentially so as not to detract from the figure of the king. In January 1682, for instance, the Moroccan ambassador watched a 'general touch' at Whitehall, after which he apologized to Charles in some embarrassment for not having presented him with a more extravagant diplomatic gift on his arrival. Having evidently been briefed that Charles was a relatively minor prince, the Moroccan ambassador now 'found him to be the greatest monarch in Europe' following this display of divine powers.[21] More alarmingly, when Charles's eldest son, the Duke of Monmouth, exploited his uncle's unpopularity during the Exclusion Crisis by undertaking a quasi-royal progress through Wiltshire, Somerset and Devon in the summer of 1680, it was reported in the London press that Monmouth had 'touched for the king's evil' as a means of promoting his authentically royal lineage and rival claim to succeed as king.

The fact that Charles's illegitimate son was seeking to claim divine sanction only reinforces the Restoration's inherent paradoxes. During the coronation service, the placing of a ring on the king's finger was intended to symbolize both the sovereign's religious faith and his marriage to his realm. But medieval theories of the monarch's 'two bodies' – the body natural and the body politic – risked derailment during the Restoration as serial adultery, extensive bastardy and wanton decadence raised concerns about the 'health' of the body politic as represented by the royal court. Accompanying the 'Bawdy House Riots' that erupted in 1668 were satirical broadsides such as *The Whores' Petition* in which London's prostitutes acclaimed the Countess of Castlemaine as the patron saint of their trade. Following Castlemaine's conversion to Catholicism in 1663, the royal court could thereby be portrayed as an expensive popish brothel. Although Charles's overt sexuality and numerous offspring proclaimed an energetic virility and fecundity that contrasted sharply with Puritan prudishness, relocating the traditional epithet of 'Merry Monarch' to its original literary context was less flattering. In verses unintentionally seen by Charles in 1674 – which resulted in their author's immediate expulsion from court – John Wilmot, Earl of Rochester, dubbed him 'The easiest king and best-bred man', observing 'His sceptre and his prick are of a length'. But 'Restless he rolls about from whore to whore, / A merry monarch scandalous and poor'.[22] While fornication and adultery were forbidden by the country's civil and canon laws, the king allegedly underwent a 'mock marriage' to one mistress, the Duchess of Portsmouth, in 1671, and Charles remains unique among British monarchs in the extent to which he flaunted his sexual conquests in ways that constantly verged on parodying royal ceremonial. The aristocratic titles and riches conferred on his numerous illegitimate offspring also effectively created a rival ducal caste that was not only expensive to maintain, but also offered alternative means of access to royal influence.

To some extent, the chorus of moral condemnation directed at Charles's court simply reflected popular disappointment. The eager optimism that had accompanied the Restoration, anticipating the re-establishment of a vigorous and fertile royal line, gradually faded in the face of a barren marriage, increasing numbers of bastard offspring, and carnal hedonism. In an early example of bacchanalian excess, 'Court wits' Charles Sackville (later Earl of Dorset) and Sir Charles Sedley appeared on a Covent Garden balcony in July 1663 and, stripped naked, delivered a mock sermon, imitated a swindler selling aphrodisiacs, washed their penises in wine, publicly defecated and threw bottles of urine on to what Pepys described as the 'thousand people standing underneath to see and hear' such antics. Although aristocratic privilege gave Sackville immunity from prosecution, Sedley was tried and fined £500; borrowing the money from Charles, Sedley became – as he put it – 'the first man that paid for shitting'.[23]

By the mid 1660s, therefore, with natural calamities of plague and fire ascribed to divine disapproval, policy failures and military defeats were increasingly attributed to the dissipation of royal energies in decadent directions. In July 1667, for instance, the Dean of Wells, Robert Creighton, preached what Pepys described as a 'strange bold sermon' before Charles 'against the sins of the court, and particularly against adultery, over and over instancing' examples from Scripture, whereby a 'whole nation was undone' by a king's infidelity, before pointedly referring to the recent and humiliating Dutch attack on the English navy in the Medway.[24] In practical terms, the sheer amount of time Charles devoted to his mistresses, together with their lavish upkeep, prompted anxiety about the insidious effects of 'petticoat government'. In 1666 and 1667 – at a time when rehousing those made homeless by the Great Fire remained an urgent priority – the king's Office of Works carried out the refurbishment of Castlemaine's apartments in the form of a painted oratory, a panelled bathroom, a bedchamber with adjacent accommodation for her children, a library lined with seven-foot-high glass-fronted bookcases, a grand staircase to a privy garden and an aviary. Destroyed by fire in the 1690s, the countess's apartments ultimately comprised twenty-four rooms and sixteen garrets which she retained after Charles's death, while her successor as principal mistress, the Duchess of Portsmouth, also occupied around the same number of rooms at Whitehall. Indeed, when Evelyn visited the duchess's apartments in 1683, he judged their luxury furnishings to have 'ten times the richness and glory' of Queen Catherine's. Admiring the 'new fabric of French tapestry ... Japanese cabinets, screens, pendulum clocks, huge vases of wrought plate, tables, stands, chimney furniture, sconces, brasses ... all of massive silver' as well as 'his Majesty's best paintings', Evelyn needed to remind himself that their acquisition had been achieved only 'with vice and dishonour'.[25] In cash receipts alone, 'secret service' payments made to the duchess from Treasury funds amounted to more than £136,000 by 1681.[26] Shortly before the anniversary of Charles I's execution that year, Gilbert Burnet's alarm at court activities prompted him to write 'a very plain letter' to the dead king's son, drawing attention to 'his past ill life, and the effects it had on the nation, with the judgements of God that lay on him', only to be later informed that, having read the letter twice, Charles 'then threw it on the fire'.[27]

Holding sway over the Restoration court in much the

same way as the male favourites of James I and VI had dominated its early seventeenth-century predecessor, Charles's mistresses operated as an independent political force. Besides offering regular access to the king, royal mistresses could act as patronage brokers, seek favours, receive diplomatic gifts ultimately intended for the monarch and provide alternative, semi-private venues for political negotiation. Particular – and justified – suspicions attached to the ambitions of Louise de Kérouaille, Duchess of Portsmouth. In October 1671 the French ambassador, Croissy, reported approvingly to one of Louis XIV's ministers that the king was now consorting with the duchess rather than 'lewd and bouncing orange girls' – namely, Nell Gwyn – and ventured that 'she has so got round King Charles as to be the greatest service to our sovereign and master, if she only does her duty'.[28] Precisely because of the duchess's Franco-Catholic affinities, however, the Duke of Monmouth preferred to meet his father at Gwyn's residence in Pall Mall. Indeed, rivalry between the king's mistresses served increasingly as a barometer for Whig and Tory attachments. In partisan polemic, the two women were pitted against one another in imaginary exchanges, with one anonymous pamphleteer presenting Gwyn as the honest, rustic English foil to her arrogant and duplicitous French rival, de Kérouaille. When the latter returned to France for three months in 1682, bearing secret messages from Charles to Louis XIV, a contemporary pamphlet imagined Gwyn bidding Portsmouth farewell and denouncing her as 'a French toadstool' who 'to foreign scents [had] betrayed the Royal Game', while 'in my clear veins, best

British blood does flow' and, rather than bankrupting the country, 'I pay my debts, [and] distribute to the poor'.[29]

In *ancien régime* France, attacks on both monarchical government and religious scepticism were often accompanied by the rejection of traditional sexual mores. In Restoration England, by contrast, the reverse held true, as allegations of monarchical tyranny at the royal court were fuelled by condemnation of its sexual libertinism and toleration of heterodox ideas. Linking Charles's amorous preferences with his political priorities, the Whig opposition produced, in June 1680, anonymous 'Articles of high treason, and other high crimes and misdemeanours' that listed twenty-two charges against the Duchess of Portsmouth, including accusations of seeking to subvert Church–State relations in England while introducing popery and tyranny; promoting an Anglo-French alliance; persuading Charles that the Popish Plot was fictitious; meddling in government and spending prodigiously. These were presumably intended to form the basis of a parliamentary attack on the duchess, but Charles refused to reconvene Parliament, obliging the Earl of Shaftesbury to present the charges to the Middlesex Grand Jury in June 1680, when the indictment was rejected by the Chief Justice, Sir William Scroggs. Denunciations of individual royal concubines thereby offered an alternative means of articulating anxieties regarding abuse of power, the persecution of Protestant nonconformists, the insidious promotion of Catholicism, and profligate extravagance.

In his posthumously published character sketch of Charles, the Marquis of Halifax observed that Charles had 'lived with his ministers as he did with his mistresses; he used them, but he was not in love with them'.[30] Charles himself contradicted this assessment when he fatalistically observed to his sister Henriette in January 1668 that were she 'as well acquainted with a little fantastical gentleman called Cupid as I am', she would appreciate the limited capacity of individuals to control their emotional affairs.[31] On that occasion, Charles was alluding to his continued infatuation with Frances Stuart, who had notoriously refused his advances before eloping with a distant cousin of the king's, another Charles Stuart, the Duke of Richmond. Charles's obsession survived their marriage, however, with Pepys recording in May that the king remained 'mighty hot upon the duchess of Richmond'. Hovering between vicarious fascination and censorious reproof, Pepys further noted that, the previous Sunday, Charles 'did on a sudden take a pair of oars or sculler, and all alone, or but one with him' rowed down the Thames to the duchess's residence in Somerset House where, 'the garden door not being open, himself clambered over the walls to make a visit to her . . . which is a horrid shame!' Earlier in his *Diary*, Pepys had been particularly prurient in following the king's tempestuous relationship with the Countess of Castlemaine. In 1662, for example, he had caught sight of her luxurious lingerie hanging out to dry and confessed that it 'did me good to look upon them', while three years later he judged one erotic nocturnal vision 'the best that ever was dreamed' in imagining holding the king's mistress in his own arms, effectively cuckolding Charles, and being 'admitted to use all the dalliance I desired with her'.[32] In addition to Charles, Castlemaine was reputed to have enjoyed love affairs with sundry conquests, including a tightrope walker, Joseph Hall, the actor Charles Hart, the playwright William Wycherley and John Churchill, later Duke of Marlborough. Based in Paris in 1678 and suspected of having started a new liaison with a French aristocrat, she wrote to Charles reminding him that 'you know, as to love, one is not mistress of one's self'.[33]

The problem for Charles was that, as king, he *was* meant to be in control of himself, but too often was instead found to have been 'unkinged' by women. In satirical poems, he was described, for instance, as 'The poor Priapus king, led by the nose' in a reference to the Greek god of fertility, famed for boasting a permanent and oversized erection.[34] Pornography and politics became inextricably linked, as illustrated by the popularity of a notorious poem entitled 'Signor Dildo'. Penned amid anxieties surrounding the Duke of York's marriage to Mary of Modena in 1673, and often attributed to the Earl of Rochester, the poem imagined 'Signor Dildo' arriving in the princess's entourage and becoming an instant favourite with the ladies at Charles II's court, being modest, discreet, permanently potent, inexpensive and disease-free. For Charles's part, although his nickname 'Old Rowley' – after a particularly prolific stallion in the royal stables – presented a backhanded compliment, in an anonymous 'Satire on Old Rowley' (1680), Charles was nevertheless advised to banish his unpopular mistresses to make 'Thy people no more doubt thee', since 'Thou are not hated, though they are'.[35]

Foreigners were equally unimpressed. Attending Charles's court in the late 1660s, the Italian diplomat Magalotti observed that Charles 'lets himself be so transported by impetuosity that in the courtesies of a lover, he forgets the decorum of a king'.[36] Moreover, as Charles became older, he also attracted jibes from younger court wits equating his reported physical impotence with political inadequacy on the international stage. In Rochester's verse satire of the king, he refers to the 'pains it costs to poor laborious Nelly' to employ 'hands, fingers, mouth and thighs' to 'raise the member she enjoys'.[37] Charles's susceptibility to feminine wiles also contrasted unfavourably with the steely resolve of Louis XIV, who specifically advised his son and heir that the time 'we devote to our love' must 'never be taken away from our affairs, because our first object must always be the preservation of our glory and of our authority'. As Louis insisted to his son, 'while surrendering our heart we remain masters of our mind' and 'keep the affections of a lover separate from the decisions of a sovereign'.[38] This was borne out more generally: in a sardonic aphorism circulating in 1681, it was recognized that 'the king of France could whore well and govern well' while 'our king could whore well but not govern'.[39] Reflecting public perceptions, Evelyn rued – on the day after Charles's death – that he would have been 'an excellent prince doubtless had he been less addicted to women'.[40]

5
Words

The Wildean adage that 'Life imitates Art far more than Art imitates Life' might well have been written with Charles II's reign in mind as the turbulent excesses of the royal court often rivalled the more exuberant antics on the Restoration stage. As Aphra Behn famously rued in the prologue to *The Feigned Courtesans* (1679): 'The Devil take this cursed plotting age, / It has ruined all our plots upon the stage' since 'Every fool turns politician now'.[1] Indeed, Charles II's return to power was inextricably associated with the re-opening of London's playhouses, after stage plays had been banned by parliamentary edict in 1642. A royal patent issued in August 1660 conferred the right to perform plays on two companies – the King's and the Duke's – forming the basis of the modern rights exercised by the Drury Lane Theatre and the Royal Opera House. The inauguration of Restoration theatre has thus been acclaimed as 'an act of state' and equivalent to the creation of the British Broadcasting Corporation in the 1920s.[2] As one contemporary playwright put it, 'The Playhouse is the nation's weather-glass',[3] for the theatre offered the irresistible opportunity to present the real-life 'dramas' – political, religious and sexual – of Charles's reign in allegorical, tragic or comedic guise. Blurring the boundary between royal ceremonial and dramatic depiction, one of the Restoration stage's most prominent actors, Thomas Betterton, twice borrowed the coronation robes worn by Charles in 1661 as theatrical costumes for plays such as Roger Boyle's *The History of Henry the Fifth* (1664), which celebrated the reassertion of English dominance in France. Later depictions of the Restoration court emphasized its theatricality and penchant for role-playing. In Sir Walter Scott's *Peveril of the Peak* (1823), for instance, an imaginary exchange between Charles II and George Villiers, 2nd Duke of Buckingham, is cut short when the king reminds Buckingham 'that we have an audience to witness this scene' and that they 'should walk the stage with dignity'.[4]

In practical terms, Charles's patronage of public theatres removed the need for his treasury to fund the production costs of lavish court entertainments, while he also enthusiastically attended plays away from London, including those 'acted in a barn, and by very ordinary Bartholomew Fair comedians' in Newmarket.[5] The monarch also exerted control over material performed, reviewing the content of forthcoming schedules with playhouse managers and discussing the plots of plays with dramatists. In the preface to his rhymed tragedy *Aureng-Zebe* (1676), John Dryden confirmed that not only had his text benefited from 'the king's perusal' before completion, but 'the most considerable event' in the drama had also been 'modelled' by Charles.[6] Having grown accustomed to watching female parts performed by women in French and

German theatres during the 1650s, Charles also transformed professional opportunities for English actresses overnight by issuing a royal patent in 1662 declaring that all female roles should henceforth be played by women. An uglier side to Charles's interest in the theatre emerged in December 1670, however, when the MP Sir John Coventry proposed a tax on playhouses in the House of Commons, only to be informed that actors were exempt from civil jurisdiction or taxation since they were 'the king's servants and a part of his pleasure'. Having then audaciously asked 'whether did the king's pleasure lie among the men or women that acted', Coventry was ambushed that evening by soldiers from the Duke of Monmouth's guard and his nose was slit to the bone.[7]

For the Restoration remained an era in which the dissemination of words was tightly controlled, whether in written or spoken form. In a sermon preached before Charles in 1662, a royal chaplain, William Haywood, insisted that seditious thoughts invariably translated into rebellious deeds, warning that 'words are the readiest instruments; words are the bellows that kindle the sparks; words are the wind that ventilates the flame'.[8] That same year, the Licensing Act made press censorship a matter of statutory authority for the first time, rather than royal prerogative. Although the Act's provisions unintentionally lapsed amid repeated parliamentary prorogations in 1679, printers and authors thereafter remained liable for prosecution for materials deemed libellous, indecent or blasphemous. In 1663, the committed loyalist Roger L'Estrange was appointed as the government's Surveyor and Licensor of the Press and, seven years later, claimed to have 'suppressed above 600 sorts of seditious pamphlets' by refusing publication licences.[9] The re-establishment of the Post Office also provided Charles's government with opportunities to intercept private correspondence, extending techniques developed by the Cromwellian intelligence system. Having developed devices to duplicate documents, open letters unobtrusively and counterfeit seals, the former Cromwellian spy-turned-Royalist Samuel Morland remained convinced that 'a skilful prince ought to make a watch tower of his General Post Office'.[10]

Since attendance at Anglican service was legally enforceable by law, the majority of Charles's subjects encountered royal government much less frequently than the established Church, where weekly sermons were the main means by which political information was disseminated. Shortly before returning from exile, Charles had been warned about the need to monitor sermon content by his former mentor, the Earl of Newcastle, who stressed the need to prevent ministers 'disputing your right and prerogative in pulpits' and attempting 'every Sunday to make libels', for 'once authority is despised, what can follow but a civil war?'[11] Instead, parish pulpits needed to become the prime conduit for upholding royal authority and maintaining civil order. Indeed, as the Oxford cleric Robert South pointed out to members of Lincoln's Inn in 1660, if there was 'not a minister in every parish, you would quickly find cause to increase the number of constables'.[12] At the Restoration, a new anniversary fast was added to the liturgical calendar to commemorate Charles I's execution on 30

January, together with a new thanksgiving feast on 29 May to celebrate his son's restoration, both of which offered annual opportunities for preachers to comment on current events by way of historical analogy. In 1685, Bishop Francis Turner of Ely claimed that over three thousand sermons commemorating the regicide were preached annually, but since there were nine thousand English parishes, the actual figure may well have been much higher.[13] As politics polarized during the 1670s – and parallels were increasingly drawn with the 1640s – loyalists warned that their opponents would always seek to conceal subversion under a cloak of religious grievance. Fearing a resurgence of 'that old deformed Hell-hag rebellion', the cleric John Higham recalled that Charles I had been 'first preached to death in the pulpit before he was put to death on the scaffold'.[14] Charles's son, however, preferred to advise his sister Henriette to follow 'the same convenience that the rest of the family has, of sleeping' through homilies, acknowledging that 'we have the same disease of sermons that you complain of' in France.[15]

The potential for church pulpits to promote monarchical authority was matched, in inverse proportion, by the destabilizing capacity of coffee houses to undermine royal power. To the caffeine-addicted city dwellers of today, urban culture of the late seventeenth century would seem reassuringly familiar on account of the popularity of commercial coffee houses, increasingly visible from around 1650. A London barber, Thomas Rugg, claimed that coffee was 'sold almost in every street' by 1659, while the natural philosopher Robert Hooke recorded visits to over sixty different London coffee houses in his diary entries for the 1670s.[16] For loyalists, however, coffee houses represented a subversive and foreign innovation that fostered popular interest in state affairs, fanning republican aspirations and encouraging conspiracy, in contrast to the rustic virtues associated with traditional alehouses, where dutiful subjects conventionally drank the monarch's health. Regarding coffee houses as the secular equivalent of Nonconformist conventicles, Charles's government repeatedly considered how to curb their seemingly insatiable appeal and, in December 1674, issued a royal proclamation setting a time limit outside of which the retail sale of coffee, chocolate, tea and sherbet would be prohibited. Although overwhelming commercial opposition forced a policy reversal, the government's concern to suppress the 'diverse false, malicious and scandalous reports' that denigrated Charles's monarchy and fomented discontent was addressed when coffee-house owners were later enjoined to ensure that only officially licensed newspapers were read on their premises and not manuscript libels.[17]

Government paranoia about the content of manuscript material in private possession mounted during the 'Tory Reaction' and was dramatically demonstrated during the treason trial of one of the Earl of Leicester's sons, Algernon Sidney. Having been convicted and sentenced to execution on evidence that included an unfinished manuscript in his possession, but without demonstrable proof of his authorship, Sidney's scaffold speech in 1683 lamented that 'we live in an age that makes truth pass for treason'. Since 'nothing of particular application unto time, place or person could be found' in his manuscripts, 'all was supplied by innuendos'. While his discourses on historical rulers, such as Tarquin, Nero, Caligula, Domitian or Hugh Capet could have been subjected to scholarly scrutiny, Sidney objected that his fate had instead been decided by a jury 'composed of men utterly unable to understand them' as judicial prosecutors became partisan literary critics.[18] In his summing-up, Judge George Jeffreys had insisted that 'scribere est agere' – to write is to act.

Although Charles himself attached importance to 'the word of a king' in royal undertakings, he penned no extensive writings, as his grandfather James I and VI had done, and often prefaced personal letters by admitting 'the natural laziness I have towards writing'.[19] His prose was, however, characteristically witty, ironic and direct. While he was engaged in acrimonious negotiations with the Scottish Covenanters in 1650, for instance, a letter issued in Charles's name self-consciously appropriated his adversaries' canting language by inviting the Committee of Estates to attend him in Perth, trusting 'that the Lord will return again, that hath smitten us, and will bless our consultations'.[20] Charles's own account of his experiences while on the run from his enemies after the Battle of Worcester was likewise wryly self-deprecating. Recalling the need to stop at a Bromsgrove blacksmith, the disguised monarch was asked by the smith 'if that rogue, Charles Stuart' had yet been captured. In response, Charles had ventured that 'if that rogue were taken, he deserved to be hanged more than all the rest' for having invaded England with an army of Scottish supporters, to which the blacksmith had confirmed 'that I spoke like an honest man'.[21] Safely removed from Presbyterian disdain while he was in exile, his correspondence with an Irish courtier, Theobald Taafe, discussed recurrent romantic intrigues – in which Charles pseudonymously referred to himself as 'Don Lauren' – and vividly recounted daily distractions in Bruges, such as going to 'eat pancakes and draw Valentines with the women' on Shrove Tuesday in 1657.[22] It was, however, precisely such blithe insouciance that made senior Royalists doubt the likelihood of his imminent restoration. James Butler, Duke of Ormonde, confided his fear to Hyde the following year that Charles's 'immoderate delight in empty effeminate and vulgar conversations' had 'become an irresistible part of his nature' and a fatal distraction.[23] As king, however, Charles remained an entertaining conversationalist with what Evelyn described as 'a particular talent in telling stories', especially 'facetious passages of which he had numerable'.[24] Charles's physician, Welwood, likewise recalled numerous animated discussions, acknowledging that 'when he had a mind to lay aside the king, there was a thousand irresistible charms in his conversation'.[25]

Candour was also evident in Charles's formal speeches to Parliament and in his royal declarations and proclamations, a much higher proportion of which were printed as official state documents than had been the case for previous British monarchs. For, as Charles's government recognized, one irreversible legacy of the mid-century civil wars was increased popular interest in state affairs and the concomitant onus this placed on rulers to appeal rhetorically to the public as adjudicators. As seen in the extracts from royal publications included in Chapter 2 above, Charles repeatedly explained policy, justified his actions, appealed for support and reassured his subjects throughout his reign. Oratorical bluntness was equally evident in the strategically shrewd Declaration of Breda in 1660 as in Charles's refusal, more than twenty years later, 'to let myself be intimidated' during the Oxford Parliament when he allegedly informed the Whig peer Shaftesbury – in a conversation later reported to Louis XIV by the French ambassador in London, Paul Barillon – that whereas most 'men become ordinarily more timid as they grow old', he intended to become 'on the contrary, bolder and firmer'.[26] In 1681, a compilation of royal speeches and declarations was also published by an Inner Temple lawyer Edward Cooke to present Charles's subjects with an opportunity 'to hear him give his own royal word' against numerous misrepresentations and libels.[27]

The imprimatur attached to official publications could not, however, guarantee their veracity and, on occasion, Charles certainly lied. In a speech to both Houses of Parliament in January 1674, and subsequently printed, the king requested further funds to continue fighting the Dutch, insisting that he was not 'in love with war, for war's sake'. Furthermore, Charles claimed, his recent discussions with the French court had 'been very strangely misrepresented to you as if there were certain secret articles of dangerous consequence'. Referring only to the 'sanitized' version of the Treaty of Dover that had been publicly signed in December 1670, he wanted to 'assure you there is no other treaty with France, either before or since, not already printed, which shall not be made known'.[28] Although this speech ran to just over a hundred words in length – and could only have taken around a minute to read aloud – one peer who had observed the king's demeanour throughout reported to the Irish lord lieutenant, Arthur Capel, Earl of Essex, that although the speech had been 'the consultation of many days and nights', Charles had 'fumbled in delivering it, and made it worse than in the print', making his claims simply 'incoherent'.[29] Two years earlier, the Venetian ambassador in Madrid had received reports relating 'the peculiar behaviour of his Britannic Majesty', describing Charles's 'simulated goodwill' and disingenuity in trying 'to extort from parliament the satisfaction he claims and, that done, [will] change his tune'.[30]

As suspicions mounted among members of the opposition that Charles's public pronouncements belied his inner thoughts, manuscripts of 'mock' royal speeches started circulating, including one in the spring of 1675 attributed to Andrew Marvell. As MP for Hull, Marvell had been listening to the king's speeches in Parliament for over a decade and brilliantly parodied Charles's habitual cadences and characteristically defensive *mea culpa* stance. In this parody, Marvell portrayed the king reassuring MPs that 'my proclamation is a true Picture of my mind' and that his incessant need for additional revenue was genuine, however much MPs might distrust his promises on other matters. Protesting that 'besides many harlots in my service, my Reformado [Catholic] Concubine lies heavy on me', 'Charles' humbly promised to effect further financial retrenchment at court, by investigating 'the late embezzlements of my dripping-pans and kitchen stuff'.[31] Another mock speech, dated March 1680 – two years after Marvell's death – likewise imagined Charles insisting to MPs that 'you know I always love to keep my oath', but advised them to grant financial supply speedily, warning them that 'upon the word of a king . . . I intend to enslave you'.[32]

Other literary attacks on Charles were presented as inversions of conventional panegyrics. Shortly after the English naval victory at the Battle of Lowestoft (1665), for example, the poet Edmund Waller drew on a Venetian genre in composing a poem that supplied instructions to an artist regarding the most appropriate commemoration of the victory. Vividly endowing events with the heroism of classical antiquity, Waller's *Instructions to a Painter* (1666) portrayed the conflict between the Dutch and English fleets in the form of an encounter between the combined forces of Mark Antony and Cleopatra against Octavian at the Battle of Actium in 31 BC to determine domination of the Roman world. As Dutch successes against the English increased, however, Waller's format was easily adapted to supply caustically satirical depictions of military incompetence, political hypocrisy and national disgrace. Among a series of rejoinders, Marvell's *Third Advice to a Painter* (1667) insisted that although 'court gazettes our triumphs tell', print would soon expose 'that lie of state', as poets dared to present Charles with uncomfortable truths concealed by venal courtiers: 'what servants will conceal and counsellors spare / To tell, the painter and the poet dare'.[33]

Marvell's dissection of Charles's failings as monarch went further in his *Last Instructions to a Painter* (1667), which, running to nearly a thousand lines, concluded with a scene in which a sleeping Charles awakes to find himself confronted by a tearful virgin, bound, gagged and humiliated. Aroused by her distress, Charles attempts rape, but is rebuffed by the apparition which the king then recognizes as the elusive 'England or the Peace', before it evaporates. Mingling punning references to coins, medals, prostitutes ('pieces') and politics, Marvell's *Last Instructions* underlined Charles's perceived inability to distinguish erotic fantasy from state affairs, with additional resonance arising from the fact that his *desirée*, Frances Stuart, had posed as 'Britannia' for a commemorative medal earlier that year in an image reproduced on the Royal Mint's fifty-pence coins between 1969 and 2008 and on two-pound coins from 2015 (see picture 8).

By the time of the Popish Plot, political drama had moved to the streets as increasingly elaborate 'pope burning' processions were organized – whereby an effigy of the pope was carried through the City of London behind a long parade of people dressed as Catholic clergy – at poignant political junctures or on anniversaries, such as that commemorating Elizabeth I's accession in November 1558. Particularly popular among Charles's Whig opponents, they could entail substantial expenditure and draw enormous crowds: one procession staged in November 1679 involved a papal effigy that cost £100 while newspaper reports claimed that two hundred thousand spectators witnessed its burning at Temple Bar.[34] In playhouses, dramatists produced topical adaptations of William Shakespeare's history plays, finding contemporary echoes in his depictions of civil war, rebellion and mob rule, together with themes of monarchical succession, disputed paternity, tyranny and abdication. Having staged an adaptation of *Titus Andronicus* during 'the pretended Popish Plot', for example, Edward Ravenscroft acknowledged the play's capacity to confirm 'the treachery of villains, and the mischiefs carried on by perjury, and false evidence'. Upholding drama's didactic role, Ravenscroft maintained that 'when ill manners and ill principles reign in a state, it is the business of the stage, as well as pulpits, to declaim and instruct'.[35] In 1680 and 1681, John Crowne staged an adaptation of *Henry VI*, the first part of which made explicit that Humphrey, Duke of Gloucester had been murdered by Catholics – not evident in Shakespeare's original – on the grounds that, as Catholics had carried 'many things that belong to the stage into the church', Crowne was justified in 'bringing what belongs to the church upon the stage'.[36] The second part was tellingly subtitled *The Misery of Civil War*, with implied parallels drawn between an increased romantic role for Edward IV (Charles II) and his ambitious French, Catholic queen, Margaret of Anjou (the Duchess of Portsmouth). In 1681, Nahum Tate expressed frustration that his adaptation of *Richard II* had been refused a performance licence, denying that 'a history of those times should be suppressed as a libel upon ours'.

Although Tate insisted that there was 'not one altered page but what breathes loyalty', government censors had presumably feared that the play could be interpreted as defending tyrannicide and that Tate's portrayal of Richard II as a royal martyr might be analogously applied to both Charles I and Charles II.[37]

Following his sudden dissolution of the Oxford Parliament, Charles became the focus of one of the seventeenth century's most complex allegorical poems: Dryden's *Absalom and Achitophel* (1681). Since his restoration, Charles had often been compared to King David from the Book of Samuel – either admiringly in terms of his return to power after a lengthy exile, or disapprovingly in the light of his adultery – but Dryden, as Charles's Poet Laureate, was the first to relocate Exclusionist politics to a biblical time 'before polygamy was made a sin', which enabled Charles/David's sexual energy to be celebrated for having 'scattered his Maker's image through his land' without moral transgression.[38] In Scripture, retribution for David's sin in arranging for his mistress's husband to be killed takes the form of a rebellion by his favourite son, Absalom, although Absalom is later betrayed and killed, leaving David a grieving king. In Dryden's rhymed retelling, the pitfalls resulting from national ingratitude, parental indulgence and royal mercy become a means to justify Charles's reassertion of monarchical authority.

Dryden's admiration for Charles's kingship was further developed in an opera, *Albion and Albanius*, co-written with Louis Grabu and rehearsed at court in May and December 1684, when it was watched by Charles. Having started as an allegorical prologue to a projected opera about King Arthur and the ancient roots of English monarchy – at a time when Charles's new palace was being built at Winchester – the three-act opera instead developed the prologue and avoided classical or mythological allegory by making its two protagonists Charles (Albion) and the Duke of York (Albanius). Providing an operatic narrative of political events between 1678 and 1683, the parts of the king and his brother were played by singers who ventriloquized their words and articulated royal thoughts and actions in an innovative form of sung dialogue. Following Charles's death in February 1685, the opera had a short run in London before performances ceased amid the national emergency caused by Monmouth's Rebellion in June.

Numerous panegyrical odes, elegies and commemorative sermons paid posthumous tribute to Charles II's clemency, liberality and generosity. In *A Loyal Tear Dropped on the Vault* (1685), Henry Anderson reminded readers that, when confronting his father's enemies in 1660, Charles 'could have crushed them with the hand of greatness' rather than granting indemnities, although Anderson's hyperbolic description of the late king as 'an angel clothed in flesh' and 'a model of heaven made up in clay' may have strained credulity.[39] Repeated reference was also made to the noon-day star that had appeared at Charles's birth in 1630, confirming the birth of Christ's 'infant brother', while other eulogies recalled the king's miraculous escape from Worcester and the day he 'lay coffined up within the Royal Tree' at Boscobel before returning as king in 1660.[40] For most authors, however, Charles's crowning legacy was simply his success in retaining his thrones and leaving his kingdoms at peace on his death; as Edmund Arwaker's poem *The Vision* (1685) put it, Charles had been his subjects' treasured 'shelter in all dangerous times and things'.[41]

6

Afterlives

Writing a monarch's life brings with it the unavoidable temptation to make categorical judgements and pass pithy sentence on whether particular kings and queens were 'Good', 'Bad', 'Misunderstood', 'Tragic' or some other broad stereotype. In an incomplete letter from 1935, the philosopher Isaiah Berlin admitted enjoying an (unidentified) satirical account of monarchs receiving university degrees in which, as he recalled to a colleague, 'Victoria would be viva'd for a First, and not get it', while Charles II would simply receive 'a Second'.[1] More recently, Ronald Hutton observed of three weighty studies of Charles published during the 1930s, by Sir George Clark, Sir Keith Feiling and David Ogg, that 'all awarded him a lower second class', playfully suggesting that the consistently disparaging verdicts of academic historians might reflect their having identified in Charles's notorious aversion to paperwork, indolent joviality and short-term opportunism habits tellingly reminiscent of 'their more irritating university students'.[2] Ironically, however, Charles II was just as prone to supply snap judgements himself. As the Marquis of Halifax later recalled, the king's esteemed 'wit' largely reflected 'the quickness of his apprehension' which 'made him find faults, and that led him to short sayings' about individuals that were not always fair 'but often very good'. For Halifax, monarchs remained in an unenviable position, however, precisely because of the burden of popular hope: 'being set upon a pinnacle ... they are exposed to censure if they do not do more to answer men's expectations than corrupted nature will allow'.[3]

The disputed right of James II and VII to have succeeded his brother as king inevitably endowed initial appraisals of Charles's reign with a tacit endorsement of the Stuarts' divinely ordained and hereditary right to rule. In his *Compendious View of the Late Tumults and Troubles in This Kingdom* (1685), James Wright welcomed proposed tributes to Charles in the form of 'statues of marble and triumphal arches', but maintained that a more fitting mark of respect would be for his former subjects to show unqualified fidelity to James as their new king.[4] Acclaiming Charles's lively character as such that 'even dullness itself would treat of wittily', Aurelian Cook in his *Titus Britannicus* (1685) likewise exhorted loyalty to James, while fondly proclaiming his late brother's royal court to have been as splendid as that of the Roman emperor Augustus, and asserting that it had been during Charles's reign 'that wit did first reign here, and appeared on the stage, as on a throne'.[5]

In early 1686, however, James II and VII ordered the publication of *Two Papers Written by the Late King Charles II*, which purportedly confirmed his brother's conviction that the Catholic Church was the true church of Christ and that divinely ordained monarchs could recast the national church as they wished. Since news of Charles's deathbed conversion to Catholicism had not circulated widely, it was only on publication of the *Two Papers* – which James claimed to have found among his brother's possessions after his death – that Charles's religious affinities came under scrutiny. Whether the *Two Papers* were a forgery or whether they accurately reflected Charles's religious beliefs has long been debated, but their appearance only increased the Church of England's opposition to James's measures to promote the cause of his Catholic co-religionists. Additionally, the priest who had attended Charles on his deathbed, Huddleston, published an account in 1688 of the king's flight from Worcester in 1651, claiming that Charles had wistfully admired aspects of Catholic worship while on the run. Amid mounting interest in Charles's conversion, new conspiracy theories alleged that impatient factions close to James had ultimately resorted to poison and 'did administer the fatal dose which sent King Charles II a going'.[6] Moreover, after James's political authority speedily unravelled in 1688, retrospective claims were made regarding Charles's own apprehensiveness about his brother's suitability to succeed him. Writing during the 1690s, Burnet reported that he had directly heard Charles express fears that, as king, James would prove 'so restless and violent that he could not hold it for four years to an end'.[7] A former ambassador to Brussels, Sir Richard Bulstrode, likewise recounted walking from Whitehall to Hyde Park with Charles in 1683 when the king had confessed himself 'weary of travelling' and 'resolved to go abroad no more'. Charles had, however, been anxious that 'when I am dead and gone, I know not what my brother will do' and had ominously predicted that 'when my brother comes to the crown, he will be obliged to leave his nations' soil'.[8]

Clandestine intrigue became central to an increasingly popular genre of 'secret histories' that sought to expose the sordid nature of Stuart aspirations to absolutism. In his salacious *Secret History of the Reigns of Charles II and James II* (1690), John Phillips rued that Charles's charisma had dangerously dazzled 'the eyes of the doting politicians of that age' before denouncing the former king as a fornicator and rapist. Invoking celestial imagery, Phillips claimed that Charles should 'have shone like the north star in the firmament of royalty', but had instead proved a 'sovereign *ignis fatuus*' that had tried 'to pollute and infect the people with all manner of debauchery and wickedness'.[9] Elsewhere, satirical 'histories', such as the anonymous *Eikon Basilike Deutera* (1694), purported to relate events from Charles's perspective, presenting him as an inveterate schemer who consulted astrology, envied Louis XIV, admitted success 'in the conquest of women, but not of men', was frustrated that 'my seeming neutrality enrages the bigots of all parties against me' in religious affairs and hoped his subjects might not suspect he had 'acted the hypocrite from my cradle'.[10] In his best-selling poem *The True-Born Englishman* (1701), Daniel Defoe alleged that, throughout his 'long, lazy, lascivious reign', Charles had 'carefully repeopled us again' by producing sufficient bastards to ensure that, within a couple of generations' time, their descendants would 'half the House with English

Peers supply'.[11] In time, Defoe's prediction proved accurate for, even though Charles was undermined politically by his failure to produce a legitimate heir, the descendants of his illegitimate offspring now feature prominently in Britain's modern aristocracy and include Princes William and Harry, via their mother's Spencer ancestry. Defoe later returned to the Restoration era in his novel *Roxana* (1724), which included a cameo appearance for Charles II and evoked memories of Nell Gwyn in its heroine's description of herself as 'the Protestant whore'.

From the 1690s onwards, vituperative attacks on the lasciviousness of Charles's court, its flagrant disregard for traditional morality and its suspected promotion of religious scepticism resonated with a wider 'moral revolution' under William and Mary that promoted Puritanical piety. For although focusing on Charles's private life and his flamboyant court deflected attention away from political threats posed by his deathbed conversion, the fact that his subjects had subsequently ejected James II and VII from the throne, in favour of James's daughter and son-in-law, rendered appraisals of his reign susceptible to Jacobite inflection. As the Duke of Buckingham admitted in his life of Charles, published in 1694, 'there's scarcely any party who speak moderately of him; but do either exceed in his praise or dispraise'.[12] Incensed by a history of England ostensibly written by 'a learned and impartial hand' – later identified as the Whiggish cleric White Kennett – the lawyer Roger North attacked Kennett's partisan portrayal of Charles for trying to 'persuade folk that his happy reign was no more than a Neronian tyranny, and that Nero-like,

he burned his own capital city'.[13] North's Jacobitism, however, ensured that his painstaking dissection of Kennett's
history remained unpublished during his lifetime for fear
of Whig reprisals, while a 'histori-tragi-comi ballad opera'
entitled *The Restoration of King Charles II, or the Life
and Death of Oliver Cromwell* was refused a performance
licence in 1732 on the grounds that the events it depicted
were too recent. In his *History of England* (1778) David
Hume acknowledged that 'the different lights' of Charles's
personality prompted 'different and even opposite senti-
ments' but identified indolence as the reason why, as king,
he had been so 'negligent of the interests of the nation,
careless of its glory, averse to its religion, jealous of its liberty, lavish of its treasure, [and] sparing only of its blood'.[14]
Promoting Whig ideals of political liberty in Britain and
the American colonies, Thomas Hollis was far more con-
demnatory in his attack on 'that riot-prince Charles the
Second', implying that he was 'a living oxymoron of disor-
derly order: a carnival lord of misrule'.[15] Equally censorious
was the late eighteenth-century Whig statesman Charles
James Fox, who opined that 'upon the whole, Charles the
Second was a bad man and a bad king', although he counselled against demonization and temptations to 'adopt
false or doubtful imputations, for the purpose of making
him a monster'.[16]

The torrent of Whig denunciation continued to flow
unabated in Lord Macaulay's *History of England* (1848),
which claimed that, once initial 'intoxication of loyalty' in
1660 had evaporated, Charles's subjects found themselves
'sold to a foreign, a despotic, a Popish court . . . and placed

under the rule of pandars and buffoons'.[17] Again, however, Whiggish waspishness only provoked retaliation from rival Tory historians, such as John Wilson Croker, who attacked Macaulay for creating a 'species of carnival history' and, deploring 'the squandering of so much melodramatic talent', concluded that Macaulay was 'a great painter but a suspicious narrator'.[18] By the early twentieth century, 'one can almost hear the net curtains twitching' in the description of Charles II supplied by Macaulay's great-nephew G. M. Trevelyan.[19] Describing the king's 'thick, sensuous lips, dark hair and face of a type more common in southern Europe', Trevelyan judged Charles's ancestry and temperament 'in every way opposite to those of the English squire who had grown up among the Puritans of Huntingdon' – Cromwell, in other words. While conceding that, during the final years of his reign, Charles was 'one of the greatest politicians' in English history, Trevelyan remained frustrated that 'even then, half his art was to prevent his adversaries from discovering till too late that he had any political ability at all'.[20]

As Trevelyan's rhetorical flourishes confirm, character portraits have always, to some extent, relied on imaginative reconstruction. In the 1690s, Buckingham hoped that the literary shortcomings of his account of Charles would be counterbalanced by his subject's inherent geniality in the same way that amateurish portraits of cherished relatives were more often admired than 'the best piece of Raphael'.[21] In the visual arts, although Benjamin West's painting *The Landing of Charles II at Dover* was selected for exhibition at the Royal Academy in 1783 on account of its commemorating a moment of historic national importance, by the Victorian era increasingly prudish and misogynistic censure was directed at the flaunted debauchery on display in works from the Restoration period. In the 1660s, Sir Peter Lely had painted a series of sensuous portraits of around ten female favourites, including the Countess of Castlemaine and Frances Stuart, which later became known as the 'Windsor Beauties' and are now displayed at Hampton Court Palace. Viewing the 'Beauties' in the 1820s, however, the critic William Hazlitt insisted that they 'look just like what they were – a set of kept mistresses, painted, tawdry, showing off their theatrical or meretricious airs and graces, without one touch of real elegance or refinement, or one spark of sentiment to touch the heart'.[22]

In a more light-hearted vein, Charles II's reign could be construed simply as a spirited costume drama – evident in the 'Restoration Ball' that Queen Victoria and Prince Albert hosted at Buckingham Palace in 1851; while the narrative painter Edward Matthew Ward used Evelyn's diary to conjure *An Interview between Charles II and Nell Gwynne, as Witnessed by Evelyn* (1854), which now hangs in the Victoria and Albert Museum. In prose fiction, Sir Walter Scott's novel *Peveril of the Peak* (1823), set during the Popish Plot, emphasized the king's sundry personae, variously presenting Charles as a refined monarch, consummate actor and charismatic scallywag, and – three years later – Scott's *Woodstock, or the Cavalier* (1826) retold the dramatic story of Charles's flight from Worcester for a new generation. Following several nineteenth-century novels set in the Restoration, J. M. Barrie's play *Peter Pan and Wendy* (1904) relocated Charles to seasonal pantomime by describing the villain, Captain Hook, when he first appeared, as 'cadaverous and black-avised, his hair dressed in long curls which look like black candles about to melt', while 'in dress he apes the dandiacal associated with Charles II'.[23]

Only two years before *Peter Pan* appeared, however, the lay Catholic theologian and poet G. K. Chesterton had written a biographical essay on Charles II, insisting that he was not, as too often assumed, 'a pantomime king', nor indeed 'the aimless flâneur'. Chesterton's Charles was, rather, 'a patient and cunning politician' who disguised his sagacity 'under so perfect a mask of folly that he not only deceived his allies and opponents, but has deceived almost all the historians that have come after him'. Charles's natural scepticism was encapsulated in the mysterious motives later ascribed to his deathbed conversion to Catholicism. According to Chesterton, since for Charles 'the wafer might not be God; similarly it might not be a wafer', conversion to Catholicism 'consummated the last great act of logical unbelief'.[24]

Following the First World War, a new generation discovered escapism in the irresistible exuberance of the Restoration court and 'Charles became the royal patron of the Roaring Twenties' with six biographies published between 1924 and 1933.[25] In their wildly successful parody of school history, *1066 and All That* (1930), W. C. Sellar and R. J. Yeatman had asserted that, although civil war Cavaliers might have been 'Wrong but Wromantic', their Parliamentarian enemies had been 'Right but Repulsive'.[26] In a biography of Charles entitled *Old Rowley* (1933), the right-wing writer and crime novelist Dennis Wheatley likewise presented himself as having 'survived the arctic-douche of school-taught history' during which Charles's character had been relentlessly 'belittled' in a centuries-old attempt to discredit Jacobitism. Wheatley confidently prophesied, however, that 'the day will come, when Charles will take his rightful place in history, as the wise, sweet-natured king who led his people out of darkness, anarchy and persecution' into enlightened prosperity and civilization. Drawing explicit contemporary parallels, Wheatley insisted that 'in the pyjama and bottle parties, the night clubs, and the doings of the "bright young people" of the early 1920s, we see reflected the licence of the Restoration'.[27]

Easily the most popular biography of this era was, however, Arthur Bryant's *Charles II* (1931), which went through seven impressions in eighteen months, totalling 27,000 copies.[28] As the interwar generation saw their countryside threatened by ceaseless industrialization and urbanization, Bryant's depiction of late seventeenth-century England offered a nostalgically rustic antidote. Penning a preface to the second edition in 1955, Bryant acknowledged that, although *Charles II* had been written when he was in his early thirties and was thus 'a young man's book ... full of fire and enthusiasm', he remained convinced that Charles 'came near to being a genius, was a brilliant politician, a wit, a shrewd philosopher of life, and a brave, highly intelligent and charming man'.[29] Given the overtly right-wing political views espoused by both Wheatley and Bryant during the 1930s, their admiration for the charismatic leadership of a past monarch has unmistakable ideological overtones. Equally admiring of Charles II's 'subtlety and genius for negotiation' was the Anglo-French Catholic writer Hilaire Belloc, who enjoyed a sustained literary collaboration with Chesterton. Entitled *The Last Rally: A Story of Charles II* (1940), Belloc's biography denounced 'Whiggery' for the way it 'took the story of England and told it in its own terms, suppressed what it would, told what lies it felt inclined to tell, and at last made them all pass – the suppressions and the falsehoods – as current coin'.[30]

Interest in Charles II was not, however, the exclusive preserve of those on the political right. While teaching at a preparatory school in Middlesex in 1932, Eric Blair – who later adopted the pen name George Orwell – wrote a two-act play entitled 'King Charles II' for his pupils. Set towards the end of Charles's flight from Worcester, the play articulated a popular nostalgia for a strong monarchical ruler and gave an early indication of Orwell's subsequent distrust of revolutionary governments.[31] Seven years later, a play by the ardent socialist George Bernard Shaw, *'In Good King Charles's Golden Days': A True History that Never Happened*, was first performed at the Malvern Festival in August 1939, less than a month before Britain entered the Second World War. Set in Isaac Newton's putative home in Cambridge, the play's action takes place over a single imagined day in 1680. In the first act, Newton receives an unexpected visit from a 'very tall and very dark' man, with 'a lot of dogs', going under the name of 'Mr Rowley' (Charles), together with the Quaker George Fox and, in due course, the Duke of York, Godfrey Kneller, the Countess of Castlemaine, the Duchess of Portsmouth and Nell Gwyn. The second act is set in the same day, but in Queen Catherine's 'boudoir' in Newmarket, and involves only Charles and Catherine. Writing with comfortable hindsight, Charles warns his brother, York, that although 'I keep the crown by my wits', he fears James would be so unsuitable a successor that it might 'not be far kinder of me to push the Exclusion Bill through' to save him from their father's fate. As Charles fears, 'they will have your head off inside of five years unless you jump into the nearest fishing smack and land in France'. Later, to Catherine, Charles ruefully concedes that, since 'no-one can govern the English', it was 'the worst of luck to be born a king'.[32]

Increased international tension during the 1930s also inspired the production of stirringly patriotic historical drama on celluloid. Starring the director's future wife, Anna Neagle, as the movie's eponymous heroine, Herbert Wilcox's *Nell Gwyn* (1934) was one of the first British films to enjoy extensive commercial success in the United States, although only after government censors had insisted on appending a moralizing prologue to a film packed with ribald double entendres and an epilogue showing Gwyn in eventual destitution after Charles's death (see picture 15). To prepare for her role, Neagle evidently read numerous history books, visited museums and force-fed herself porridge and milk to achieve the desired Restoration voluptuousness, while the

film presented Charles as a worldly-wise and generous
monarch whose liaison with Gwyn confirmed his unusual
facility to transcend conventional class boundaries.

By the second half of the twentieth century, the cleavage
between popular and academic approaches to Charles II
had become entrenched. Generally admiring accounts of
the king, embracing his popular appeal, were produced by
Lady Antonia Fraser and Richard Ollard in the 1970s, to
be followed by detailed and largely hostile critiques by
Ronald Hutton and John Miller in the 1980s.[33] For his
part, Hutton confessed the extent to which he had found
several years 'working constantly upon a monarch whom
I disliked, and with an atmosphere of intrigue and inse-
curity which I found uncongenial, genuinely depressing'.[34]
Describing Charles as 'monumentally selfish', Hutton
insisted that 'at his core lay a vacuum'; the king was a man
with 'a set of strongly marked characteristics [but] with a
cold void at the centre'.[35] Having intended to produce a
definitive academic interpretation that drew detailed attention to Charles's shortcomings as a monarch, Hutton was
depressed by the persistence of popular stereotypes and –
ultimately, it seemed – defeated in his aim. Objecting to the
benign portrayal of the king in the BBC television series
Charles II: The Power and the Passion (2003), Hutton
later admitted that 'I really believed that the work of John
Miller and myself in the 1980s and 1990s might finally have
killed off the 1920s legend of Charles II by revealing a
monarch so unpleasant that he could never be made a cred-
ible hero again'.[36]

My own biographical meditation ends on a more

positive note. Charles II was certainly a conflicted character and a compulsive dissimulator: he was a monarch of multiple masks. Yet Charles's complexity was not only a product of the endemic instability of the political world that he inherited and in which he operated, but also appeals to modern interests in the psychological make-up of prominent individuals and the presentational spin deployed by those in power to conceal personal vulnerabilities. In the late 1770s, the French Enlightenment *philosophe* Denis Diderot proposed what later became known as 'Diderot's Paradox' by maintaining that the best dramatic performances were those achieved by actors who refused to identify with a fictional character or project their own personality when playing a role, deploying instead calculated deliberation to produce an interpretation that was consistent and technically accomplished. As Diderot insisted, a 'man of feeling' would 'never be a great king, a great minister, a great general, a great advocate or a great doctor'. At 'the least unexpected thing', Diderot warned, 'the man of feeling loses his head'.[37] Charles II was neither a thoroughgoing 'man of feeling' nor a consistently cool operator who strategically secured all his interests, but, unlike his father, he did not lose his head and, unlike his brother, he did not lose his thrones.

Notes

1. THE STAR KING

1. Ronald Hutton, *Charles II: King of England, Scotland and Ireland* (Oxford: Clarendon Press, 1989), p. 458.
2. H. C. Foxcroft (ed.), *A Supplement to Burnet's History of My Own Time* (Oxford: Clarendon Press, 1902), p. 48; [John Sheffield, Duke of Buckingham], *The character of Charles II, King of England. With a short account of his being poisoned* (London: Richard Baldwin, 1696), p. 9.
3. John Miller, *Charles II* (London: Weidenfeld & Nicolson, 1991), p. xiii; Rachel Weil, 'The Female Politician in the Late Stuart Age', in Julia Marciari Alexander and Catharine MacLeod (eds), *Politics, Transgression, and Representation at the Court of Charles II* (London: Yale University Press, 2007), p. 183; and Stephen Coote, *Royal Survivor: The Life of Charles II* (London: Yale University Press, 1999), p. xi.
4. 'A Character of King Charles II', in Mark N. Brown (ed.), *The Works of George Savile, Marquis of Halifax*, 3 vols (Oxford: Oxford University Press, 1989), II, p. 499.
5. 'The Earl of Newcastle's Letter of Instruction to Prince Charles for His Studies, Conduct and Behaviour', in Henry Ellis (ed.), *Original Letters Illustrative of English History*, 11 vols (London: Harding, Triphook & Lepard, 1824–46), III, p. 290.
6. John Spurr, *England in the 1670s: 'This Masquerading Age'* (Oxford: Blackwell, 2000), p. 2.
7. Robert Herrick, 'A Pastoral upon the Birth of Prince Charles', in Tom Cain and Ruth Connelly (eds), *The Complete Poetry of Robert Herrick*, 2 vols (Oxford: Oxford University Press, 2013), I, p. 82; for evidence that the poem was written at the time of Charles's birth, and not subsequently, see II, p. 226.
8. Sir Audley Mervin, *A speech made by Sir Audley Mervin, His Majesties prime serjeant at law in Ireland* (Dublin: 1661), p. 7.
9. S. Elliott Hoskins, *Charles the Second in the Channel Islands*, 2 vols (London: R. Bentley, 1854), II, p. 324.
10. *His Majesties Most Gracious Speech to both Houses of Parliament . . . on Thursday the 13 of September, 1660* (London: John Bill and Christopher Barker, 1660), p. 13.
11. Ruth Norrington (ed.), *My Dearest Minette: The Letters between Charles II and His Sister Henrietta, Duchesse d'Orléans* (London: Peter Owen, 1996), p. 108.
12. James VI and I, 'Basilicon Doron', in J. P. Sommerville (ed.), *King James VI and I: Political Writings* (Cambridge: Cambridge University Press, 1994), p. 13.

13. Quoted in Gerard Reedy, 'Mystical Politics: The Imagery of Charles II's Coronation', in Paul J. Korshin (ed.), *Studies in Change and Revolution: Aspects of English Intellectual History, 1640–1800* (Menston: Scolar Press, 1972), p. 29.
14. Walter Charleton, *A Character of His Most Sacred Majesty, Charles the Second* (London: H. Herringman, 1661), p. 10; Charles Patin, *Rélations historiques et curieuses des voyages, en Allemagne, Angleterre, Hollande, Bohême, Suisse* (Amsterdam: P. Mortier, 1695), p. 173.
15. Jonathan Scott, *Seventeenth-Century English Political Instability in European Context* (Cambridge: Cambridge University Press, 2000), p. 26.
16. George Bernard Shaw, *'In Good King Charles's Golden Days'*, in *The Bodley Head Collected Plays with Their Prefaces*, 7 vols (London: Bodley Head, 1970–74), VII, p. 251.

2. LIFE

1. 'Earl of Newcastle's Letter of Instruction', in Ellis (ed.), *Original Letters*, III, pp. 288–9.
2. Edward, Earl of Clarendon, *The History of the Rebellion: A New Selection*, ed. Paul Seaward (Oxford: Oxford University Press, 2009), p. 126.
3. Edward, Earl of Clarendon, *The History of the Rebellion, and Civil Wars in England Begun in the Year 1641*, ed. W. Dunn Macray, 6 vols (Oxford: Clarendon Press, 1888), III, p. 449.
4. Ibid., IV, pp. 168–9.
5. Hutton, *Charles II*, p. 33.
6. *Diary of Alexander Jaffray, Provost of Aberdeen, One of the Scottish Commissioners to Charles II* (London: Harvey, 1833), p. 32.
7. David Laing (ed.), *Correspondence of the Earls of Ancram and Lothian*, 2 vols (Edinburgh: 1875), II, p. 497*.
8. Robert Douglas, *The Form and Order of the Coronation of Charles the II, King of Scotland, together with the Sermon then Preached, by Mr Robert Douglas* (Aberdeen: James Brown, 1660), pp. 25, 15.
9. R. Scrope and T. Monkhouse (eds), *State Papers collected by Edward, Earl of Clarendon, commencing from the year 1621*, 3 vols (Oxford: Clarendon Printing House, 1767–86), III, p. 562.
10. See http://www.dailymail.co.uk/home/moslive/article-1374494/Red-Lion-White-Hart-Most-popular-pub-names-England.html (accessed 12 February 2015).
11. Sir Arthur Bryant (ed.), *The Letters, Speeches and Declarations of King Charles II* (London: Cassell, 1968), p. 60.
12. Ibid., p. 33.
13. 'Declaration of Breda, 1660', in Andrew Browning (ed.), *English Historical Documents. Volume VI: 1660–1714* (London: Eyre & Spottiswoode, 1953), p. 57.
14. Scrope and Monkhouse (eds), *State Papers collected by Edward, Earl of Clarendon*, III, p. 745.
15. Alan Macfarlane (ed.), *The Diary of Ralph Josselin 1616–1683* (Oxford: Oxford University Press for the British Academy, 1991), pp. 457–8.
16. E. S. de Beer (ed.), *The Diary of John Evelyn*, 6 vols (Oxford: Clarendon Press, 1955), III, p. 246.

17. *An act for a perpetuall anniversary thanksgiving on the nine and twentieth day of May* (1660), 12 car. 11, c. 14.

18. Bryant (ed.), *Letters, Speeches and Declarations*, p. 114.

19. Robert Latham and William Matthews (eds), *The Diary of Samuel Pepys*, 11 vols (London: Bell, 1971), V, p. 46.

20. Quoted in Thomas P. Slaughter, *Ideology and Politics on the Eve of Restoration: Newcastle's Advice to Charles II* (Philadelphia: American Philosophical Society, 1984), p. 52.

21. 'Declaration of Breda, 1660', in Browning (ed.), *English Historical Documents*, p. 58.

22. Bryant (ed.), *Letters, Speeches and Declarations*, p. 114.

23. Ibid., p. 112.

24. Ibid., p. 126.

25. Ibid., pp. 120–21.

26. De Beer (ed.), *Diary of John Evelyn*, III, p. 457.

27. Bryant (ed.), *Letters, Speeches and Declarations*, p. 193.

28. [Joseph Glanvill], *A loyal tear dropped on the vault of our late martyred sovereign* (London: E. Cotes, 1667), p. 23.

29. Latham and Matthews (eds), *Diary of Samuel Pepys*, VIII, p. 181, and IX, p. 132.

30. Jacques Truchet (ed.), *Orations funèbres de Bossuet* (Paris: Gallimard, 1961), pp. 126–7.

31. Quoted in Barbara Shapiro, *John Wilkins, 1614–1672: An Intellectual Biography* (Berkeley, Calif.: University of California Press, 1969), p. 187.

32. H. M. Margoliouth (ed.), *The Poems and Letters of Andrew Marvell*, 3rd edn, 2 vols (Oxford: Clarendon Press, 1971), II, p. 317.

33. Gilbert Burnet, *History of My Own Time*, ed. Osmund Airy, 2 vols (London: 1897–1900), I, pp. 492–3.

34. Norrington (ed.), *My Dearest Minette*, pp. 165, 170.

35. Latham and Matthews (eds), *Diary of Samuel Pepys*, IX, p. 536.

36. Quoted in Norrington (ed.), *My Dearest Minette*, p. 212.

37. Bryant (ed.), *Letters, Speeches and Declarations*, p. 247.

38. Allen B. Hinds (ed.), *Calendar of State Papers and Manuscripts Relating to English Affairs, Existing in the Archives and Collections of Venice. Volume XXXVIII: 1673–1674* (London: HMSO, 1940 [1947]), p. 321.

39. Anon., *A Letter from a Person of Quality to his Friend in the Country* ([London]: 1675), pp. 2, 29.

40. Quoted in Mark Knights, *Representation and Misrepresentation in Later Stuart Britain: Partisanship and Political Culture* (Oxford: Oxford University Press, 2005), p. 36n.

41. [Andrew Marvell], *An Account of the Growth of Popery and Arbitrary Government in England* (Amsterdam: 1677), pp. 127, 1, 14.

42. [Roger L'Estrange], *An account of the Growth of Knavery, under the pretended fears of Arbitrary Government and Popery. With a parallel betwixt the Reformers of 1677, and those of 1641, in their methods, and designs* (London: 1678), p. 46.

43. Bryant (ed.), *Letters, Speeches and Declarations*, p. 299.

44. Ibid., p. 331.

45. Ibid., p. 317.

46. Ibid., p. 321.

47. Charles II, *His Majesties Gracious Letter to his Parliament of Scotland* (London: Thomas Newcomb, 1681), p. 7.

48. James Welwood, *Memoirs of the most material transactions in England, for the last hundred years, preceding the Revolution of 1688* (London: Timothy Goodwin, 1700), p. 138.
49. De Beer (ed.), *Diary of John Evelyn*, IV, p. 413–14.

3. IMAGE

1. Mary Anne Everett Green (ed.), *Letters of Henrietta Maria Including Her Private Correspondence with Charles the First* (London: R. Bentley, 1857), p. 17.
2. 'The King's Own Account', in William Matthews (ed.), *Charles II's Escape from Worcester: A Collection of Narratives Assembled by Samuel Pepys* (London: Bell, 1967), p. 54.
3. Quoted in Anna Keay, *The Magnificent Monarch: Charles II and the Ceremonies of Power* (London: Continuum, 2008), p. 48.
4. Quoted in Eva Scott, *The Travels of the King: Charles II in Germany and Flanders, 1654–1660* (London: A. Constable, 1907), p. 458.
5. Quoted in Christine Stevenson, *The City and the King: Architecture and Politics in Restoration London* (New Haven, Conn.: Yale University Press, 2013), p. 82.
6. Sir Samuel Tuke, *A character of Charles the Second, written by an impartial hand, and exposed to publick view for information of the people* (London: G. Bedell, 1660), p. 5.
7. Richard Flecknoe, *Heroic Portraits: with other miscellary [sic] pieces, made and dedicated to his Majesty* (London: Ralph Wood, 1660), sig. Bv.
8. 'Character', in Brown (ed.), *Works of George Savile*, II, pp. 490, 486.
9. W. E. Knowles Middleton (ed.), *Lorenzo Magalotti at the Court of Charles II: His Relazione d'Inghilterra of 1668* (Waterloo, Ont.: Wilfred Laurier University Press, 1980), p. 28.
10. Welwood, *Memoirs*, p. 131.
11. I Chronicles 29:23.
12. David H. Solkin, 'Isaac Fuller's *Escape of Charles II*: A Restoration Tragicomedy', *Journal of the Warburg and Courtauld Institutes*, 62 (1999), p. 211.
13. 'The Notebooks of George Vertue Relating to Artists and Collections in England: Volume IV', *Walpole Society*, 20 (1931–2), p. 120; 24 (1937–8), p. 28.
14. [John Evelyn], *Sculptura: or the history and art of chalcography and engraving in copper* (London: J[ames] C[ottrell], 1662), p. 26.
15. Allen B. Hinds (ed.), *Calendar of State Papers and Manuscripts Relating to English Affairs, Existing in the Archives and Collections of Venice. Volume XXXVII: 1671–2* (London: HMSO, 1939), p. 221.
16. [Henry Stubbe], *A Justification of the Present War against the United Netherlands* (London: Henry Hills & John Starkey, 1672), p. 40.
17. Quoted in B. J. Rahn, 'A *Ra-Ree Show* – A Rare Cartoon: Revolutionary Propaganda in the Treason Trial of Stephen College', in Korshin (ed.), *Studies in Change and Revolution*, p. 89.
18. Horace Walpole, *Ædes Walpolianæ: or, A Description of the Collection of Pictures at Houghton-Hall in Norfolk* (London: 1747), p. xvi.
19. Richard Baxter, 'Preface' to Jacques Boileau, *A Just and Seasonable Reprehension of Naked Breasts and Shoulders* (London: Jonathan Edwin, 1678), sigs A6v, A7v.

20. David Piper, *The English Face* (London: Thames & Hudson, 1957), p. 96; quoted in Philip Mansel, *Dressed to Rule: Royal and Court Costume from Louis XIV to Elizabeth II* (New Haven, Conn.: Yale University Press, 2005), p. 50.
21. 'A Dialogue between the Two Horses', in Margoliouth (ed.), *Poems and Letters of Andrew Marvell*, I, p. 212.
22. Sir John Lauder of Fountainhall, *Historical Notices of Scottish Affairs*, ed. David Laing, 2 vols (Edinburgh: T. Constable, 1848), II, p. 635.
23. See http://webapps.fitzmuseum.cam.ac.uk/explorer/index.php?qu=charles%20ii%20AND%20%28Material:terracotta%20OR%20Technique:terracotta%29&oid=29779 (accessed 16 March 2016).
24. Nicholas Barbon, *An Apology for the Builder: Or, A Discourse showing the Cause and Effects of the Increase of Building* (London: Cave Pullen, 1685), p. 33.
25. Simon Thurley, 'A Country Seat Fit for a King: Charles II, Greenwich and Winchester', in Eveline Cruickshanks (ed.), *The Stuart Courts* (Stroud: Sutton, 2000), p. 226.
26. John Evelyn, 'Dedication', in Roland Fréart de Chambray, *A parallel of the ancient architecture with the modern* (London: T. Roycroft, 1664), sigs A2v–A3r.
27. Quoted in Stevenson, *The City and the King*, pp. 19–20.
28. Quoted in Michael Hunter, 'The Making of Christopher Wren', *London Journal*, 16 (1991), p. 101.
29. John Evelyn, *London Revived: Considerations for its Rebuilding in 1666*, ed. E. S. de Beer (Oxford: 1938), pp. 54–5.
30. Latham and Matthews (eds), *Diary of Samuel Pepys*, VIII, p. 497.
31. Charles's souvenir ticket is now in the Museum of London; see G. Croom, *Frost Fair Keepsake for King Charles II* (London: G. Croom, 1684).

4. MAJESTY

1. 'Earl of Newcastle's Letter of Instruction', in Ellis (ed.), *Original Letters*, III, p. 290.
2. Quoted in Kevin Sharpe, *Rebranding Rule: The Restoration and Revolution Monarchy, 1660–1714* (New Haven, Conn.: Yale University Press, 2013), p. 149.
3. Latham and Matthews (eds), *Diary of Samuel Pepys*, VII, p. 201; see Keay, *Magnificent Monarch*, p. 3.
4. Thomas Bruce, Earl of Ailesbury, *Memoirs, Written by Himself*, ed. W. E. Buckley, 2 vols (Westminster, London: Nichols & Son, 1890), I, p. 87.
5. 'Earl of Newcastle's Letter of Instruction', in Ellis (ed.), *Original Letters*, III, p. 290.
6. Latham and Matthews (eds), *Diary of Samuel Pepys*, I, p. 158; II, pp. 157–8.
7. Colley Cibber, *An Apology for the Life of Colley Cibber, Comedian, and Late Patentee of the Theatre-Royal* (London: John Watts, 1740), p. 19.
8. Andrew Browning (ed.), *Memoirs of Sir John Reresby: The Complete Text and a Selection from His Letters* (London: Offices of the Royal Historical Society, 1991), p. 259.
9. F. H. Blackburne Daniell (ed.), *Calendar of State Papers, Domestic Series, January to November, 1671* (London: HMSO, 1895), p. 392.
10. Hutton, *Charles II*, p. 133.
11. Ailesbury, *Memoirs*, I, p. 87.

12. Scrope and Monkhouse (eds), *State Papers collected by Edward, Earl of Clarendon*, III, p. 174.
13. Keay, *Magnificent Monarch*, p. 74.
14. Ibid., p. 107.
15. Latham and Matthews (eds), *Diary of Samuel Pepys*, III, p. 297.
16. De Beer (ed.), *Diary of John Evelyn*, II, p. 333; IV, p. 42.
17. Latham and Matthews (eds), *Diary of Samuel Pepys*, II, p. 88.
18. Quoted in Anna Keay, '"Toyes and Trifles": The Destruction of the English Crown Jewels', *History Today*, 52 (July 2002), p. 37.
19. John Browne, 'Charisma Basilicon', in *Adenochoiradelogia, or, An Anatomick-Chirurgical Treatise of Glandules & Strumaes, or King's-Evil-swellings* (London: Thomas Newcomb, 1684), III, p. 156.
20. Mark 16:18.
21. Quoted in Keay, *Magnificent Monarch*, p. 119.
22. John Wilmot, Earl of Rochester, 'A Satire on Charles II', in Joseph Black et al. (eds), *The Broadview Anthology of British Literature. Volume 3: The Restoration and the Eighteenth Century*, 2nd edn (Peterborough, Ont.: Broadview, 2012), p. 291.
23. Latham and Matthews (eds), *Diary of Samuel Pepys*, IV, p. 209; Andrew Clark (ed.), *The Life and Times of Anthony Wood, Antiquary, of Oxford, 1632–1691, Described by Himself. Volume 1: 1632–1660* (Oxford: Clarendon Press, 1891), p. 477.
24. Latham and Matthews (eds), *Diary of Samuel Pepys*, VIII, p. 362.
25. De Beer (ed.), *Diary of John Evelyn*, IV, p. 74.
26. Nancy Klein Maguire, 'The Duchess of Portsmouth: English Royal Consort and French Politician, 1670–1685', in R. Malcolm Smuts (ed.), *The Stuart Court and Europe: Essays in Politics and Political Culture* (Cambridge: Cambridge University Press, 1996), p. 265.
27. Burnet, *History of My Own Time*, II, p. 299.
28. Quoted in Alan Marshall, *The Age of Faction: Court Politics, 1660–1702* (Manchester: Manchester University Press, 1999), p. 192.
29. Anon., *A Dialogue, between the Dutchess of Portsmouth, and Madam Gwin, at parting* (London: 1682), pp. 1–2.
30. 'Character', in Brown (ed.), *Works of George Savile*, II, p. 493.
31. Norrington (ed.), *My Dearest Minette*, p. 143.
32. Latham and Matthews (eds), *Diary of Samuel Pepys*, IX, p. 205, III, p. 87, and VI, p. 191.
33. Quoted in Sonya Wynne, '"The Brightest Glories of the British Sphere": Women at the Court of Charles II', in Catherine MacLeod and Julia Marciari Alexander (eds), *Painted Ladies: Women at the Court of Charles II* (London: National Portrait Gallery, 2001), p. 44.
34. Anon., 'An Historical Poem (1680)', in Elias F. Mengel (ed.), *Poems on Affairs of State: Augustan Satirical Verse, 1660–1714. Volume 2: 1678–1681* (New Haven, Conn.: Yale University Press, 1965), p. 158.
35. Anon., 'Satire on Old Rowley (1680)' in Mengel (ed.), *Poems on Affairs of State*, p. 186.
36. Knowles Middleton (ed.), *Lorenzo Magalotti*, p. 28.
37. Rochester, 'A Satire on Charles II', in Black et al. (eds), *Broadview Anthology of British Literature*, pp. 291–2.
38. Paul Sonnino (ed. and trans.), *Mémoires for the Instruction of the Dauphin* (New York: Free Press, 1970), pp. 246–7.

39. Quoted in Grant Tapsell, *The Personal Rule of Charles II, 1681–1685* (Woodbridge: Boydell, 2007), p. 45.

40. De Beer (ed.), *Diary of John Evelyn*, IV, p. 410.

5. WORDS

1. Aphra Behn, *The Feign'd Curtizans, or A Night's Intrigue* (London: J. Tonson, 1679), sig. Á4r.

2. Susan J. Owen, *Restoration Theatre and Crisis* (Oxford: Clarendon Press, 1996), p. 16.

3. Nahum Tate, *The Ingratitude of a Commonwealth; Or, The Fall of Laius Martius Coriolanus* (London: 1682), p. 64.

4. Sir Walter Scott, *Peveril of the Peak*, ed. Alison Lumsden (Edinburgh: Edinburgh University Press, 2007), p. 326.

5. Browning (ed.), *Memoirs of Sir John Reresby*, p. 259.

6. John Dryden, *Aureng-Zebe: A Tragedy* (London: 1676), sig. A4v.

7. Margoliouth (ed.), *Poems and Letters of Andrew Marvell*, II, p. 321.

8. William Haywood, *A sermon dissuading from Obloquy against Governors preached on Sunday December 7 1662 ... and now ... made public* (London: J. G[rismond], 1663), p. 1.

9. Mary Anne Everett Green (ed.), *Calendar of State Papers Domestic Series, 1670* (London: HMSO, 1895), p. 502.

10. Quoted in Alan Marshall, *Intelligence and Espionage in the Reign of Charles II, 1660–1685* (Cambridge: Cambridge University Press, 1994), p. 81.

11. Slaughter (ed.), *Ideology and Politics*, p. 17.

12. Robert South, *Ecclesiastical Policy the best Policy: Or, Religion the best Reason of State* (Oxford: 1660), p. 7.

13. Quoted in Helen Randall, 'The Rise and Fall of a Martyrology: Sermons on Charles I', *Huntington Library Quarterly*, 10 (1947), p. 136.

14. [John Higham], *A Looking Glass for Loyalty: or, The Subjects Duty to his Sovereign* (London: Henry Brome, 1675), sig. A8r, p. 120.

15. Norrington (ed.), *My Dearest Minette*, p. 73.

16. Steve Pincus, ' "Coffee Politicians Does Create": Coffeehouses and Restoration Political Culture', *Journal of Modern History*, 67 (1995), p. 812.

17. Charles II, *A Proclamation for the suppression of Coffee-houses* (London: John Bill and Christopher Barker, 1675), p. 1; Brian Cowan, 'The Rise of the Coffeehouse Reconsidered', *Historical Journal*, 47 (2004), p. 29.

18. Algernon Sidney, *The very copy of a Paper delivered to the Sheriffs upon the scaffold on Tower-hill on Friday, December 7, 1683* (London: 1683), pp. 1, 3.

19. Bryant (ed.), *Letters, Speeches and Declarations*, p. 65; Norrington (ed.), *My Dearest Minette*, p. 160.

20. Laing (ed.), *Correspondence of the Earls of Ancram and Lothian*, II, p. 499*.

21. 'The Kings Own Account', in Matthews (ed.), *Charles II's Escape from Worcester*, p. 52.

22. Timothy Crist (ed.), *Charles II to Lord Taafe: Letters in Exile* (Cambridge: Rampant Lions, 1974) p. 23.

23. Scrope and Monkhouse (eds), *State Papers collected by Edward, Earl of Clarendon*, III, p. 387.

24. De Beer (ed.), *Diary of John Evelyn*, IV, p. 410.

25. Welwood, *Memoirs*, p. 130.

26. W. D. Christie, *A Life of Anthony Ashley Cooper, First Earl of Shaftesbury*, 2 vols (London: Macmillan, 1871), II, p. cxvi.

27. Edward Cooke, *Memorabilia; or, The most remarkable Passages and Counsels collected out of the several Declarations and Speeches that have been made by the King* (London: Nevil Simmons, 1681), sig. B2r.

28. *His Majesties Most Gracious Speech, together with the Lord Keeper's, to both Houses of Parliament, January 7, 1673/4* (London: John Bill and Christopher Barker, 1674), pp. 3–4.

29. Quoted in Annabel Patterson, *The Long Parliament of Charles II* (New Haven, Conn.: Yale University Press, 2008), p. 82.

30. Hinds (ed.), *Calendar of State Papers . . . Venice, 1671–2*, p. 21.

31. [Andrew Marvell], 'His M—s most gracious Speech to both Houses of P—t' [1675], in *Poems on Affairs of State, from 1640 to this present year 1704, Written by the greatest wits of the age*, vol. III ([?London]: 1704), pp. 86, 85, 87.

32. Quoted in Patterson, *Long Parliament*, p. 90.

33. Andrew Marvell, 'The Third Advice to a Painter', in *Poems on Affairs of State: Augustan Satirical Verse, 1660–1714. Volume 1: 1660–1678*, ed. George deF. Lord (New Haven, Conn.: Yale University Press, 1963), pp. 74, 87.

34. Tim Harris, *London Crowds in the Reign of Charles II : Propaganda and Politics from the Restoration until the Exclusion Crisis* (Cambridge: Cambridge University Press, 1987), p. 104.

35. Edward Ravenscroft, *Titus Andronicus, or The Rape of Lavinia* (London: 1687), sigs A2r–A2v.

36. John Crowne, *Henry the Sixth, the First Part* (London: R. Bentley & M. Magnes, 1681), sig. A4r.

37. Nahum Tate, *The History of King Richard the Second* (London: R. Tonson & J. Tonson, 1681), sigs Ar, A2v.

38. John Dryden, 'Absalom and Achitophel', in Paul Hammond and David Hopkins (eds), *Dryden: Selected Poems* (Harlow: Pearson/Longman, 2007), p. 159.

39. Henry Anderson, *A Loyal Tear dropt on the Vault of the High and Mighty Prince Charles II of glorious and happy memory* (London: Luke Meredith, 1685), pp. 19, 13.

40. Sir F[rancis] F[ane], *A Pindarick Ode on the Sacred Memory of our late Gracious Sovereign Charles II* (London: J. Playford, 1685), p. 4; 'J. H.', *A Pindarick Ode on the Death of his late Sacred Majesty King Charles II of Blessed Memory* (London: 1685), p. 2.

41. Edmund Arwaker, *The Vision: A Pindarick Ode occasioned by the death of our late gracious Sovereign, King Charles II* (London: J. Playford, 1685), p. 3.

6. AFTERLIVES

1. Isaiah Berlin, *Flourishing: Letters 1928–1946*, ed. Henry Hardy (London: Chatto & Windus, 2004), p. 145.

2. Ronald Hutton, *Debates in Stuart History* (Basingstoke: Palgrave Macmillan, 2004), pp. 136–7.

3. 'Character', in Brown (ed.), *Works of George Savile*, II, pp. 495, 505.

4. James Wright, *A Compendious View of the late Tumults and Troubles in this Kingdom by way of annals for seven years* (London: Edward Jones, 1685), p. 208.

5. Aurelian Cook, *Titus Britannicus: an essay of History Royal, in the Life and Reign of his late sacred Majesty, Charles II* (London: James Partridge, 1685), sigs A7r, B4r.

6. [Sheffield, Duke of Buckingham], *Character of Charles II*, sig. Cr.

7. Burnet, *History of My Own Time*, ed. Airy, II, p. 409.

8. Sir Richard Bulstrode, *Memoirs and Reflections upon the Reign and Government of King Charles the First and King Charles the Second* (London: N. Mist, 1721), p. 424.

9. [John Phillips], *The Secret History of the Reigns of Charles II and James II* (n.p.: 1690), pp. 3, 25.

10. Anon., *Eikon Basilike Deutera: The Pourtraicture of His Sacred Majesty King Charles II* (n.p.: 1694), pp. 125, 258, 297.

11. [Daniel Defoe], *The True-Born Englishman: A Satire* ([London: 1701]), pp. 17–18.

12. [Sheffield, Duke of Buckingham], *Character of Charles II*, sigs B3r–B3v.

13. Roger North, *Examen: or, an Enquiry into the credit and veracity of a pretended complete history* (London: F. Gyles, 1740), 'Preface', p. i.

14. David Hume, *The History of England from the Invasion of Julius Caesar to the Revolution in 1688*, ed. William B. Todd, 6 vols (Indianapolis: Liberty Fund, 1983), VI, p. 447.

15. Quoted in James Grantham Turner, *Libertines and Radicals in Early Modern London: Sexuality, Politics and Literary Culture* (Cambridge: Cambridge University Press, 2002), p. 165.

16. Charles James Fox, *Sketches of the Characters of Charles I and II and Oliver Cromwell* (London: Effingham Wilson, 1839), p. 39.

17. Thomas Babington Macaulay, *The History of England from 1485 to 1685*, ed. Peter Rowland (London: Folio Society, 1985), p. 262.

18. Quoted in William Thomas, *The Quarrel of Macaulay and Croker: Politics and History in the Age of Reform* (Oxford: Oxford University Press, 2000), pp. 296–7.

19. Kevin Sharpe, ' "Thy Longing Country's Darling and Desire": Aesthetics, Sex and Politics in the England of Charles II', in Alexander and MacLeod (eds), *Politics, Transgression, and Representation*, p. 21.

20. George Macaulay Trevelyan, *England Under the Stuarts* (London: Folio Society, 1996), pp. 294, 314.

21. [Sheffield, Duke of Buckingham], *Character of Charles II*, p. 2.

22. Quoted in Julia Marciari Alexander, 'Beauties, Bawds and Bravura: The Critical History of Restoration Portraits of Women', in MacLeod and Alexander (eds), *Painted Ladies*, p. 65.

23. J. M. Barrie, *Peter Pan and Other Plays*, ed. Peter Hollindale (Oxford: Clarendon Press, 1995), p. 108.

24. G. K. Chesterton, 'Charles II', in *Twelve Types* (London: Arthur C. Humphreys, 1902), pp. 105, 95.

25. Hutton, *Debates in Stuart History*, p. 138.

26. W. C. Sellar and R. J. Yeatman, *1066 and All That* (Stroud: Sutton, 1993), p. 201.

27. Dennis Wheatley, *Old Rowley: A Private Life of Charles II* (London: Hutchinson, 1933), pp. 11, 180, 71.

28. Julia Stapleton, *Arthur Bryant and National History in Twentieth-Century Britain* (Lanham, Md.: Lexington Books, 2005), p. 59.

29. Arthur Bryant, *Charles II*, 2nd edn (London: Collins, 1955), pp. 85, viii.

30. Hilaire Belloc, *The Last Rally: A Story of Charles II* (London: Cassell, 1940), pp. 155, 231.

31. William T. Blair, 'George Orwell's "King Charles II": An Early Criticism of Revolutionary Government', *Review of English Studies*, 41 (1990), 370–73.

32. Shaw, *'In Good King Charles's Golden Days'*, pp. 214, 248, 293, 295–6.

33. Antonia Fraser, *Charles II* (London: Weidenfeld & Nicolson, 1979); Richard Ollard, *The Image of the King: Charles I and Charles II* (London: Hodder & Stoughton, 1979); Hutton, *Charles II* ; Miller, *Charles II*.

34. Hutton, *Debates in Stuart History*, p. 157.

35. Hutton, *Charles II*, p. 458.

36. Ronald Hutton, 'Why Don't the Stuarts Get Filmed?', in Susan Doran and Thomas S. Freeman (eds), *Tudors and Stuarts on Film: Historical Perspectives* (Basingstoke: Palgrave Macmillan, 2009), p. 256.

37. Denis Diderot, 'The Paradox of the Actor', in Geoffrey Bremner (ed. and trans.), *Denis Diderot: Selected Writings on Art and Literature* (London: Penguin, 1994), p. 106.

Further Reading

The most comprehensive and deeply researched life of Charles II is Ronald Hutton's *Charles II: King of England, Scotland and Ireland* (Oxford: Clarendon Press, 1989), which should be the first port of call for readers wishing to explore further the fascinating life of this unusual monarch. For Hutton's candid insights into his often frustrating experiences of writing the king's biography, see his article, 'Charles II', in Hutton, *Debates in Stuart History* (Basingstoke: Palgrave Macmillan, 2004), pp. 132–70. More narrowly focused on Charles II as monarch of England is John Miller's *Charles II* (London: Weidenfeld & Nicolson, 1991), while Paul Seaward's *Oxford Dictionary of National Biography* entry on Charles II supplies a clear and detailed chronological narrative (http://www.oxforddnb.com/index/5/101005144/). Jenny Uglow's *A Gambling Man: Charles II and the Restoration, 1660–1670* (London: Faber & Faber, 2009) provides an accessible account of Charles's first decade of kingship, while contemporary accounts of his dramatic flight to the continent in 1651 are collated in William Matthews (ed.), *Charles II's Escape from Worcester* (London: Bell, 1967). A lively sense of Charles's personality emerges in the collection of letters between Charles and his cherished sister Henriette, edited by Ruth Norrington and entitled *My Dearest Minette: The Letters between Charles II and His Sister Henrietta, Duchesse d'Orléans* (London: Peter Owen, 1996), while Sir Arthur Bryant's edited collection *The Letters, Speeches and Declarations of King Charles II* (London: Cassell, 1968) is also valuable.

There is no modern biography of Charles's queen, Catherine of Braganza, but an insightful introduction is available in Edward

Corp's 'Catherine of Braganza and Cultural Politics', in Clarissa Campbell Orr (ed.), *Queenship in Britain, 1660–1837: Royal Patronage, Court Culture and Dynastic Politics* (Manchester: Manchester University Press, 2002), pp. 55–73. The political, artistic and cultural dimensions to Charles's complex private life – encompassing serial mistresses and a sexually charged court culture – are knowledgeably discussed in specialist contributions to two volumes, jointly edited by Julia Marciari Alexander and Catherine MacLeod: *Painted Ladies: Women at the Court of Charles II* (London: National Portrait Gallery, 2001) and *Politics, Transgression, and Representation at the Court of Charles II* (London: Yale University Press, 2007). Anna Keay's *The Magnificent Monarch: Charles II and the Ceremonies of Power* (London: Continuum, 2008) brings to life the elaborate ceremonial of Caroline court culture, while the elusive subject of Charles's religious beliefs is discussed in Hutton's chapter, 'The Religion of Charles II', in R. Malcolm Smuts (ed.), *The Stuart Court and Europe: Essays in Politics and Political Culture* (Cambridge: Cambridge University Press, 1996), pp. 228–46. The numerous and rich visual, literary and dramatic representations of Charles's reign are exhaustively covered in the final part of Kevin Sharpe's monumental trilogy on representations of monarchical authority from Henry VIII to Queen Anne, which was posthumously published as *Rebranding Rule: The Restoration and Revolution Monarchy, 1660–1714* (New Haven, Conn.: Yale University Press, 2013). Susan J. Owen's *Restoration Theatre and Crisis* (Oxford: Clarendon Press, 1996) focuses on the political dimensions of drama performed, especially during the 'Popish Plot', and attempts to exclude Charles's Catholic brother, James, from the succession, while Christine Stevenson's *The City and the King: Architecture and Politics in Restoration London* (London: Yale University Press, 2013) is a beautifully illustrated and authoritative study of the physical transformation of London during the reign. Broader histories of Restoration Britain include Gary de Krey, *Restoration and Revolution in Britain: Political Culture in the*

Era of Charles II and the Glorious Revolution (Basingstoke: Palgrave Macmillan, 2007); Tim Harris, *Restoration: Charles II and His Kingdoms, 1660–1685* (London: Allen Lane, 2005); and George Southcombe and Grant Tapsell, *Restoration Politics, Religion and Culture: Britain and Ireland, 1660–1714* (Basingstoke: Palgrave Macmillan, 2010); while N. H. Keeble's *The Restoration: England in the 1660s* (Oxford: Blackwell, 2002) and John Spurr's *England in the 1670s: 'This Masquerading Age'* (Oxford: Blackwell, 2000) offer skilfully evocative accounts of single decades.

Often, however, the most telling and lively insights into Charles's personality and the nature of his reign may be gleaned from the immediate impressions of contemporary diarists. The eleven volumes of *The Diary of Samuel Pepys*, edited by Robert Latham and William Matthews (London: Bell, 1971), remain the best-known account of Restoration life and are handsomely complemented by Claire Tomalin's biography, *Samuel Pepys: The Unequalled Self* (London: Viking, 2002). Less intimate and more formal is the six-volume *Diary of John Evelyn*, edited by E. S. de Beer (Oxford: Clarendon Press, 1955), which, like Pepys's *Diary*, is available in various other editions and abridgements, and, again, enhanced by an excellent biography, Gillian Darley's *John Evelyn: Living for Ingenuity* (London: Yale University Press, 2006). An alternative, more Puritanically inclined, narrative of the 1680s – dubbed 'a darker shade of Pepys' – may be found in a six-volume work edited by a team headed by Mark Goldie, *The Entring Book of Roger Morrice, 1677–1691* (Woodbridge: Boydell, 2007).

Picture Credits

1. Sir Anthony van Dyck, *The Three Eldest Children of Charles I*, 1635 (Royal Collection Trust © Her Majesty Queen Elizabeth II, 2015/Bridgeman Images)
2. Isaac Fuller, *Charles II Discovered by Colonel Careless and William Penderel Seated on a Tree-stump in Boscobel Wood*, *c.*1660s (© National Portrait Gallery, London)
3. *The Scots Holding their Young King's Nose to the Grindstone*, broadside, 1651 (Lebrecht Music and Arts Photo Library/ Alamy)
4. Hieronymus Janssens, *Charles II Dancing at a Ball at Court*, *c.*1660 (Royal Collection Trust © Her Majesty Queen Elizabeth II, 2015/Bridgeman Images)
5. Samuel Cooper, unfinished *ad vivum* miniature of Charles II (reproduced by permission of the Denys Eyre Bower Bequest, Chiddingstone Castle, Kent)
6. Samuel Cooper, miniature of Catherine of Braganza, 1662 (Royal Collection Trust © Her Majesty Queen Elizabeth II, 2015/Bridgeman Images)
7. Sir Peter Lely, *Barbara Palmer (née Villiers), Duchess of Cleveland, with her Son, Charles Fitzroy, as the Madonna and Child*, *c.*1664 (© National Portrait Gallery, London)
8. Silver medal commemorating the Peace of Breda, 1667 (© National Maritime Museum, London)
9. Sir Peter Lely, *Portrait of a Young Woman and Child, as Venus and Cupid*, *c.*1670s (© Christie's Images/Bridgeman Images)

10. John Michael Wright, portrait of Charles II enthroned, *c.*1661–6 (Royal Collection Trust © Her Majesty Queen Elizabeth II, 2015/Bridgeman Images)

11. Hendrick Danckerts (attr.), *Charles II Presented with a Pineapple*, *c.*1675–80 (Ham House, Surrey/The Stapleton Collection/ Bridgeman Images)

12. Charles II touching a patient for the king's evil (scrofula). Engraving by Robert White, 1684 (Wellcome Library, London)

13. Honoré Pellé, marble bust of Charles II, 1684 (© Victoria and Albert Museum, London)

14. English school, *The Frost Fair of the Winter of 1683–4 on the Thames, with Old London Bridge in the Distance*, *c.*1685 (Yale Center for British Art, Paul Mellon Collection/Bridgeman Images)

15. Cedric Hardwicke and Anna Neagle in *Nell Gwyn*, 1934 (Kobal Collection)

16. Poster from the National Portrait Gallery's *Take Another Look* marketing campaign, 2010, featuring Thomas Hawker's portrait of Charles II, *c.*1680 (© National Portrait Gallery, London/ Poster design by True North)

Acknowledgements

Writing this short biography has been a hugely enjoyable experience and I am grateful to Simon Winder for providing me with this opportunity and to Peter Robinson for its facilitation. At Penguin, I am grateful for the editorial expertise and assistance of Maria Bedford, Anna Hervé, Cecilia Mackay and Kate Parker. I am likewise indebted to Will Ferguson, Mark Goldie, Susanna Mitchell and William O'Reilly, who read this book in draft, while Amy Blakeway and Ian Campbell provided assistance with translations. *Charles II: The Star King* was commissioned shortly after completing *The Stuarts* series for BBC2 and I am warmly appreciative of the intellectual and creative stimulation provided by, among others, Richard Downes, Neil McDonald and Colin Murray at BBC Scotland. The fact that this biography was written during university term time, while serving as Trinity Hall's Senior Tutor, was only possible with practical assistance from my PA, Julie Powley, and a dedicated tutorial office team within college. In May 1664, an 'afternoon playing the good husband' was deemed sufficiently unusual for Charles II to record its occurrence in a letter to his sister Henriette. For my part, since time spent with Charles inevitably meant repeated absences from home, I am deeply grateful to Mark and Julius for their cheerful tolerance and unstinting encouragement. Additional thanks are due to Julius for helpfully pointing out the close physical resemblance between Charles and J. M. Barrie's Captain Hook.

Index

Penguin Monarchs

* Now in paperback

THE HOUSE OF TUDOR

Henry VII	Sean Cunningham
Henry VIII*	John Guy
Edward VI*	Stephen Alford
Mary I*	John Edwards
Elizabeth I	Helen Castor

THE HOUSE OF STUART

James I	Thomas Cogswell
Charles I*	Mark Kishlansky
[Cromwell*	David Horspool]
Charles II*	Clare Jackson
James II	David Womersley
William III & Mary II*	Jonathan Keates
Anne	Richard Hewlings

THE HOUSE OF HANOVER

George I	Tim Blanning
George II	Norman Davies
George III	Amanda Foreman
George IV	Stella Tillyard
William IV	Roger Knight
Victoria*	Jane Ridley

THE HOUSES OF SAXE-COBURG & GOTHA AND WINDSOR

Edward VII*	Richard Davenport-Hines
George V*	David Cannadine
Edward VIII*	Piers Brendon
George VI*	Philip Ziegler
Elizabeth II*	Douglas Hurd

* Now in paperback

ALLEN LANE
an imprint of
PENGUIN BOOKS

Also Published

Stephen Kotkin, *Stalin, Vol. II: Waiting for Hitler, 1928-1941*

Lindsey Fitzharris, *The Butchering Art: Joseph Lister's Quest to Transform the Grisly World of Victorian Medicine*

Serhii Plokhy, *Lost Kingdom: A History of Russian Nationalism from Ivan the Great to Vladimir Putin*

Mark Mazower, *What You Did Not Tell: A Russian Past and the Journey Home*

Lawrence Freedman, *The Future of War: A History*

Niall Ferguson, *The Square and the Tower: Networks, Hierarchies and the Struggle for Global Power*

Matthew Walker, *Why We Sleep: The New Science of Sleep and Dreams*

Edward O. Wilson, *The Origins of Creativity*

John Bradshaw, *The Animals Among Us: The New Science of Anthropology*

David Cannadine, *Victorious Century: The United Kingdom, 1800-1906*

Leonard Susskind and Art Friedman, *Special Relativity and Classical Field Theory*

Maria Alyokhina, *Riot Days*

Oona A. Hathaway and Scott J. Shapiro, *The Internationalists: And Their Plan to Outlaw War*

Chris Renwick, *Bread for All: The Origins of the Welfare State*

Anne Applebaum, *Red Famine: Stalin's War on Ukraine*

Richard McGregor, *Asia's Reckoning: The Struggle for Global Dominance*

Chris Kraus, *After Kathy Acker: A Biography*

Clair Wills, *Lovers and Strangers: An Immigrant History of Post-War Britain*

Odd Arne Westad, *The Cold War: A World History*

Max Tegmark, *Life 3.0: Being Human in the Age of Artificial Intelligence*

Jonathan Losos, *Improbable Destinies: How Predictable is Evolution?*

Chris D. Thomas, *Inheritors of the Earth: How Nature Is Thriving in an Age of Extinction*

Chris Patten, *First Confession: A Sort of Memoir*

James Delbourgo, *Collecting the World: The Life and Curiosity of Hans Sloane*

Naomi Klein, *No Is Not Enough: Defeating the New Shock Politics*

Ulrich Raulff, *Farewell to the Horse: The Final Century of Our Relationship*

Slavoj Žižek, *The Courage of Hopelessness: Chronicles of a Year of Acting Dangerously*

Patricia Lockwood, *Priestdaddy: A Memoir*

Ian Johnson, *The Souls of China: The Return of Religion After Mao*

Stephen Alford, *London's Triumph: Merchant Adventurers and the Tudor City*

Hugo Mercier and Dan Sperber, *The Enigma of Reason: A New Theory of Human Understanding*

Stuart Hall, *Familiar Stranger: A Life Between Two Islands*

Allen Ginsberg, *The Best Minds of My Generation: A Literary History of the Beats*

John Edwards, *Mary I: The Daughter of Time*

Grayson Perry, *The Descent of Man*

Deyan Sudjic, *The Language of Cities*

Norman Ohler, *Blitzed: Drugs in Nazi Germany*

Carlo Rovelli, *Reality Is Not What It Seems: The Journey to Quantum Gravity*

Catherine Merridale, *Lenin on the Train*

Susan Greenfield, *A Day in the Life of the Brain: The Neuroscience of Consciousness from Dawn Till Dusk*

Christopher Given-Wilson, *Edward II: The Terrors of Kingship*

Emma Jane Kirby, *The Optician of Lampedusa*

Minoo Dinshaw, *Outlandish Knight: The Byzantine Life of Steven Runciman*

Candice Millard, *Hero of the Empire: The Making of Winston Churchill*

Christopher de Hamel, *Meetings with Remarkable Manuscripts*

Brian Cox and Jeff Forshaw, *Universal: A Guide to the Cosmos*

Ryan Avent, *The Wealth of Humans: Work and Its Absence in the Twenty-first Century*

Jodie Archer and Matthew L. Jockers, *The Bestseller Code*

Cathy O'Neil, *Weapons of Math Destruction: How Big Data Increases Inequality and Threatens Democracy*

Peter Wadhams, *A Farewell to Ice: A Report from the Arctic*

Richard J. Evans, *The Pursuit of Power: Europe, 1815-1914*

Anthony Gottlieb, *The Dream of Enlightenment: The Rise of Modern Philosophy*

Marc Morris, *William I: England's Conqueror*

Gareth Stedman Jones, *Karl Marx: Greatness and Illusion*

J.C.H. King, *Blood and Land: The Story of Native North America*

Robert Gerwarth, *The Vanquished: Why the First World War Failed to End, 1917-1923*

Joseph Stiglitz, *The Euro: And Its Threat to Europe*

John Bradshaw and Sarah Ellis, *The Trainable Cat: How to Make Life Happier for You and Your Cat*

A J Pollard, *Edward IV: The Summer King*

Erri de Luca, *The Day Before Happiness*

Diarmaid MacCulloch, *All Things Made New: Writings on the Reformation*

Daniel Beer, *The House of the Dead: Siberian Exile Under the Tsars*

Tom Holland, *Athelstan: The Making of England*

Christopher Goscha, *The Penguin History of Modern Vietnam*

Mark Singer, *Trump and Me*

Roger Scruton, *The Ring of Truth: The Wisdom of Wagner's Ring of the Nibelung*

Ruchir Sharma, *The Rise and Fall of Nations: Ten Rules of Change in the Post-Crisis World*

Jonathan Sumption, *Edward III: A Heroic Failure*

Daniel Todman, *Britain's War: Into Battle, 1937-1941*

Dacher Keltner, *The Power Paradox: How We Gain and Lose Influence*

Tom Gash, *Criminal: The Truth About Why People Do Bad Things*

Brendan Simms, *Britain's Europe: A Thousand Years of Conflict and Cooperation*

Slavoj Žižek, *Against the Double Blackmail: Refugees, Terror, and Other Troubles with the Neighbours*

Lynsey Hanley, *Respectable: The Experience of Class*

Piers Brendon, *Edward VIII: The Uncrowned King*

Matthew Desmond, *Evicted: Poverty and Profit in the American City*

T.M. Devine, *Independence or Union: Scotland's Past and Scotland's Present*

Seamus Murphy, *The Republic*

Jerry Brotton, *This Orient Isle: Elizabethan England and the Islamic World*

Srinath Raghavan, *India's War: The Making of Modern South Asia, 1939-1945*

Clare Jackson, *Charles II: The Star King*

Nandan Nilekani and Viral Shah, *Rebooting India: Realizing a Billion Aspirations*

Sunil Khilnani, *Incarnations: India in 50 Lives*

Helen Pearson, *The Life Project: The Extraordinary Story of Our Ordinary Lives*

Ben Ratliff, *Every Song Ever: Twenty Ways to Listen to Music Now*

Richard Davenport-Hines, *Edward VII: The Cosmopolitan King*

Peter H. Wilson, *The Holy Roman Empire: A Thousand Years of Europe's History*

Todd Rose, *The End of Average: How to Succeed in a World that Values Sameness*

Frank Trentmann, *Empire of Things: How We Became a World of Consumers, from the Fifteenth Century to the Twenty-First*

Laura Ashe, *Richard II: A Brittle Glory*

John Donvan and Caren Zucker, *In a Different Key: The Story of Autism*

Jack Shenker, *The Egyptians: A Radical Story*

Tim Judah, *In Wartime: Stories from Ukraine*

Serhii Plokhy, *The Gates of Europe: A History of Ukraine*

Robin Lane Fox, *Augustine: Conversions and Confessions*

Peter Hennessy and James Jinks, *The Silent Deep: The Royal Navy Submarine Service Since 1945*

Sean McMeekin, *The Ottoman Endgame: War, Revolution and the Making of the Modern Middle East, 1908–1923*

Charles Moore, *Margaret Thatcher: The Authorized Biography, Volume Two: Everything She Wants*

Dominic Sandbrook, *The Great British Dream Factory: The Strange History of Our National Imagination*

Larissa MacFarquhar, *Strangers Drowning: Voyages to the Brink of Moral Extremity*

Niall Ferguson, *Kissinger: 1923-1968: The Idealist*

Carlo Rovelli, *Seven Brief Lessons on Physics*

Tim Blanning, *Frederick the Great: King of Prussia*

Ian Kershaw, *To Hell and Back: Europe, 1914–1949*

Pedro Domingos, *The Master Algorithm: How the Quest for the Ultimate Learning Machine Will Remake Our World*

David Wootton, *The Invention of Science: A New History of the Scientific Revolution*

Christopher Tyerman, *How to Plan a Crusade: Reason and Religious War in the Middle Ages*

Andy Beckett, *Promised You A Miracle: UK 80–82*

Carl Watkins, *Stephen: The Reign of Anarchy*

Anne Curry, *Henry V: From Playboy Prince to Warrior King*

John Gillingham, *William II: The Red King*

Roger Knight, *William IV: A King at Sea*

Douglas Hurd, *Elizabeth II: The Steadfast*

Richard Nisbett, *Mindware: Tools for Smart Thinking*

Jochen Bleicken, *Augustus: The Biography*

Paul Mason, *PostCapitalism: A Guide to Our Future*

Frank Wilczek, *A Beautiful Question: Finding Nature's Deep Design*

Roberto Saviano, *Zero Zero Zero*

Owen Hatherley, *Landscapes of Communism: A History Through Buildings*

César Hidalgo, *Why Information Grows: The Evolution of Order, from Atoms to Economies*

Aziz Ansari and Eric Klinenberg, *Modern Romance: An Investigation*

Sudhir Hazareesingh, *How the French Think: An Affectionate Portrait of an Intellectual People*

Steven D. Levitt and Stephen J. Dubner, *When to Rob a Bank: A Rogue Economist's Guide to the World*

Leonard Mlodinow, *The Upright Thinkers: The Human Journey from Living in Trees to Understanding the Cosmos*

Hans Ulrich Obrist, *Lives of the Artists, Lives of the Architects*

Richard H. Thaler, *Misbehaving: The Making of Behavioural Economics*

Sheldon Solomon, Jeff Greenberg and Tom Pyszczynski, *Worm at the Core: On the Role of Death in Life*

Nathaniel Popper, *Digital Gold: The Untold Story of Bitcoin*

Dominic Lieven, *Towards the Flame: Empire, War and the End of Tsarist Russia*

Noel Malcolm, *Agents of Empire: Knights, Corsairs, Jesuits and Spies in the Sixteenth-Century Mediterranean World*

James Rebanks, *The Shepherd's Life: A Tale of the Lake District*

David Brooks, *The Road to Character*

Joseph Stiglitz, *The Great Divide*

Ken Robinson and Lou Aronica, *Creative Schools: Revolutionizing Education from the Ground Up*

Clotaire Rapaille and Andrés Roemer, *Move UP: Why Some Cultures Advances While Others Don't*

Jonathan Keates, *William III and Mary II: Partners in Revolution*

David Womersley, *James II: The Last Catholic King*

Richard Barber, *Henry II: A Prince Among Princes*

Jane Ridley, *Victoria: Queen, Matriarch, Empress*

John Gray, *The Soul of the Marionette: A Short Enquiry into Human Freedom*

Emily Wilson, *Seneca: A Life*